5 CH

5 CHOICES

Own your behaviours, master your communication,
determine your success.

Louise Evans

 THE 5 CHAIRS

Praise
for Louise and '5 Chairs, 5 Choices'

"One of the most practical books on emotional intelligence that I have ever read."
Richard Barrett,
Chairman and Founder of the Barrett Values Centre.

"Louise's groundbreaking book is for anyone who is interested in bringing more empathy, emotional intelligence and consciousness into their career (and into their daily life). The examples in this insightful book are practical and easy to integrate; and it's a must-read for anyone who wants to be an inspiring and more effective Leader."
Ellen Looyen, Bestselling Author,
"Branded for Life!"

"Louise's book is masterful. It is deep and rich yet practical, packed with scenarios, examples and exercises which when applied have transformational results for individuals, teams and organisations. I predict The 5 Chairs programme will become a reference point for the organisational development industry."
Helen Battersby, Director,
Global Business Leaders Ltd.

"It takes foresight, great empathy and courage to face the challenge of bringing the spiritual experience into the business context where the primary objective of profitability can easily blur man's dignity. On reading '5 Chairs, 5 Choices', I am in awe at how Louise achieves this with disarming creativity, clarity, enlightened sensitivity and fun, all significant qualities of the true mentor that she is!"
Faye Miravite, CEO,
Miravite Consulting Group

"I am personally very happy to see this book become a reality. I had the opportunity of working with Louise in my previous job as Managing Director of the Italian branch of a Multinational company where she supported my team through a period of re-positioning when tensions were high and relations strained. The 5 Chairs programme is powerful and practical. It opened our minds and hearts and allowed us to become more vulnerable and authentic with one another in volatile and uncertain times. The impact? Our site was awarded best in class during the Lean Program Audit. I want to thank Louise for being such an influential coach, an energetic and engaging trainer and a trustful business partner."
Luca Labriola, Head of Operations,
Personal Care, Philips

"As a young manager at the beginning of my career '5 Chairs, 5 Choices' has had an enormous impact on my approach to work and to life in general. Working in the HR task force of an important international company of luxury hotels worldwide I constantly use this method to build empathy and trust towards my international colleagues. Every

time the Jackal in me declares "in Italy, we do it better", I receive an emergency call from my "Giraffe" gently whispering "in Italy, we do it differently." This immediately changes my attitude, language and approach resulting in much greater collaborative performance. I highly recommend this book to all young talents of my generation who want to make a difference with their leadership in international contexts."

Samira Amin, HR Task Force,
Mandarin Oriental Hotels

"As our world undergoes a significant transformation where we are beginning to understand the need to value the people we live and work with, tools to raise conscious awareness of ourselves and others becomes vital not only for our individual success, but increasingly for our organizational success. Louise has taken the best kernels of wisdom from masters who teach these principles on a spiritual level and has created a pathway to accessing and applying that same wisdom in our everyday lives. Her playful and creative methodology of The 5 Chairs allows transformation to happen in even the most reticent of executives and because of that she is a master in her own right!"

Monique Tallon, author of 'Leading Gracefully: A Woman's
Guide to Confident, Authentic and Effective'

"When Louise sent me her book I read it from cover to cover. Every page of her book is inspired by an ambitious desire; that we all commit to bringing the very best of ourselves in to the world in a more conscious way. The lessons of The 5 Chairs empower us to do just that. This is a must for anyone who wants to grow in this world."

Dr. Ing. Gianfranco Michelini,
Author and Entrepreneur

"I devoured Louise's book in two days, constantly visualising the story of The 5 Chairs with their zoological guests in mind. As we move from the Jackal to the Giraffe Chair the scenery and habitat changes progressively. It's like embarking on a journey across different cultures, organisations and mindsets with a simple, ingenious and exacting method which, if followed, can only lighten and enrich our daily lives."

Nicoletta Benigni, Corporate Mentor,
Trainer and Coach

"The 5 Chairs is a powerful approach to better understand how we can communicate to get the outcomes we desire. Louise draws on a vast number of sources and her own indepth insights and knowledge from many years of practice. The result is succinct, memorable and above all practical. It really works! The need has never been greater for building relationships of respect and trust at home, at work, in the wider world. The sad truth is that connectivity removes connection unless it is nurtured. Here is a long-awaited way to build (and repair) the connection we all seek."

Anne Stenbom, Director,
Global Business Leaders Ltd

Acknowledgements

My heartfelt thanks go to:

The thousands of participants who contributed to the evolution of The 5 Chairs programme.
My dear close friends who have always believed in me and encouraged me.
My coaches and mentors who have supported me with great care on this new journey.
My special team who launched me: Giancarlo, Lynn, Tess and Simone.
My brother Nick, whose pearls of wisdom constantly guide me.
And Jamal, the love of my life, who is always there for me.

Dedication

This book is dedicated to the late Marshall Rosenberg, the founder of Nonviolent Communication.
His teachings changed my life and inspired me to create The 5 Chairs.

Foreword

I have known Louise for many years and I must say that in my entire professional life there are few people I have appreciated as much as her. When we first met, her task was to improve my horrible English and it was obvious from the approach she adopted that both innovation and deep caring for the individual were her natural talents.

Louise has an anthropological spirit to her. She is not interested in the social class, role or standing of a person. She is interested in the individual as a human being and her top priority is to understand rather than judge. Her international experience, her humanistic background and her curiosity to explore the spiritual side of life, makes for quite a unique profile among the majority of trainers on the market.

Her starting point is always with the person, their behaviours and the understanding of what motivates those behaviours. Her work '5 Chairs, 5 Choices' is in many ways a synthesis of her own way of being in the world and her ability to understand the facts of life. I choose the term 'facts of life' because the book allows the reader not only to improve their individual performance at work but also at home.

In my opinion her book should be distributed to all schools. It would certainly contribute to the making of better citizens. Managers cannot reach excellence if they are not first and foremost good people and hence good citizens themselves. What Louise instills in us is the concept of accountability, a strong sense of being responsible not only for our own actions but also for other people's behaviours. If she had her way 'the Jackals' would become extinct. If everyone applied her guidelines we would live in a decidedly better world.

Careful reading of the book invites each reader to do some self-analysis. To identify which chair we are sitting on, whether we would do well to change chairs and which of the five animals we would like to emulate (the Jackal, Hedgehog, Meerkat, Dolphin, or Giraffe). It's a fascinating exercise to do especially for all those interested in self-improvement. '5 Chairs, 5 Choices' is not suitable for anyone who has chosen to sit in the sixth chair, where everything they do is right by definition and who are unprepared to challenge their own assumptions. Louise's work is for people with the intelligence and humility to believe that in life one can always improve, one can try to understand before judging and one can listen to other people's convictions no matter how diverse.

In an increasingly multicultural, globalised world where managing diversity is key to success, Louise's guidelines should be a moral obligation.

I, incidentally, have made my choice and no longer sit in the chair I believed appropriate at the beginning of my career. Furthermore, my neck has 'lengthened' because, as the giraffe teaches, seeing things from a higher vantage point greatly

helps understanding.
Thank you Louise. I am who I am today also thanks to you.

Franco Moscetti – CEO, Axel Glocal Business
and previous CEO of Amplifon Ltd

****

As we get older, many of us begin to ask ourselves one question: "What positive contribution am I making to the world with the talents I have been given, the knowledge I have absorbed and the skills I have developed?" This I believe was the question that inspired Louise on her journey to write '5 Chairs, 5 Choices.'

Louise and I have collaborated over the last 20 years in designing and delivering development projects in international organisations. What has always impressed me about Louise is her ability to create instant rapport with participants, her determination to see her own personal growth as a prerequisite to her credibility as a trainer and coach and her incredible spirit of adventure as a world traveler.

On her return from the USA after a 9-day programme on Non-Violent Communication with the late Marshall Rosenberg, I had a sense that experience would be the glue to bind her breadth of experience, learning and insight. I have since watched her craft her own voice and build this unique model from her very special mix of life experience and professional background. Several years on we can now benefit from Louise's brilliantly simple and powerful process The 5 Chairs.

The 5 Chairs is about the impact our behaviours have on the world around us. It's about how the choices we make in responding to situations define our place in the world. The 'mind tools' Louise shares in the book are practical ways to manage ourselves and others in critical conversations and I can personally vouch for the life changing impact they have on people. The 5 Chairs experience is powerful because it is somatic. The physicality of The 5 Chairs approach helps us acquire the techniques 'through the muscle' not just through our rational understanding. At the end of the book you feel more equipped, excited even, to manage your daily behaviours and conversations in a completely new way, both at work and at home. It's a real game changer.

In our work as organisational architects, we look for simple behaviours which, when spread at scale within informal networks by influential peers will create the organisational culture we aspire to work in. On reading this book I invite you to imagine what your organisation would look like if your most socially connected peers practised The 5 Chairs in their daily activity. Through a natural process of social imitation you would quickly build a culture where collaboration and innovation were the norm.

As the anthropologist, Margaret Mead, said: "never doubt that a small group of thoughtful, committed citizens can change the world. Indeed, it is the only thing that ever has." Louise, in my view, offers us a powerful and practical approach to changing the world around us, one conversation at a time. It then falls to us to organise ourselves to spread the impact of these powerful conversations in our workplaces and at home.

So, back to the question I started with. 'What positive contribution am I making to the world?' I'm sure this book will help you find the answer.

David Trickey - CEO at TCO International,
Partner at Viral Change TM, Italy

****

I first met Louise in 2005 when I became Managing Director of Manpower Group, Italy. Since then she has played a key role in helping me understand how to improve people's performance by developing their soft skills and behaviours.

I strongly believe there is a paradigm shift underway in how we work and communicate, as well as how we express, inform and entertain ourselves. Today, developing soft skills such as problem-solving, critical thinking, collaboration and communication is paramount to our success. Managing a complex organization is not easy at the best of times but with the level of change we are subject to everyday it is evermore challenging. We are seeing companies, technologies, products, cities and even countries rise and fall overnight in completely unpredictable and random ways. Businesses are more vulnerable. Technology and globalization have accelerated and intensified the natural forces of market competition. This is what we refer to in the Manpower Group as the "new normal" of instability where the only certainty is uncertainty and where new ways of working are slowly emerging.

Social skills such as emotional intelligence, influencing and collaboration are in higher demand across all industries where previously technical skills were prioritised.

With this context in mind, I believe The 5 Chairs book and training programme is extremely effective at every level of the organization. It enables CEOs to better develop themselves, senior executives become more effective leaders of their general managers and line managers become better leaders of their frontline staff.

I also believe this book is relevant for training, coaching and mentoring at any level where individuals want to improve themselves, their behaviors and their performance.

My personal experience as a leader in applying The 5 Chairs approach is that it generates more effective, more energizing and significantly more productive conversations across the organisation which consequently transforms performance.

Too often in our organisations, and in life in general, we are ineffective. Our behaviours just do not represent our intentions. The 5 Chairs will help us make the difference so needed here.

Stefano Scabbio
President Mediterranean & Southeastern Europe
Manpower Group

Introduction

Our behaviours have a huge impact in the world. They impact everything we do; the way we live, love, work, parent and lead. We know perfectly well that some of our behaviours enrich our lives and expand our happiness whilst others drain our energy and damage our relationships.

When was the last time you caught yourself misbehaving? Maybe you picked an argument with your spouse or you snapped at your children, or you said something unkind about a colleague at work or you punished yourself for making a mistake? How did that feel?

And when was the last time you were proud of your behaviour? Maybe you listened patiently to a frustrated friend as they laid bare their soul or you praised someone at the office for their work. Or maybe you forgave your spouse for blaming you for something you didn't do or you hugged someone spontaneously just to show them you love them. How did that feel?

This book is about our behaviours. The productive ones and the unproductive ones. The intentional ones and the unintentional ones. Our own and other peoples'.

We are all architects of behaviour. We generate behaviours non-stop, from the moment we get out of bed in the morning to the moment we return there at night. Sometimes consciously, often unconsciously.

Have you ever found yourself wondering 'Why did I do that?' or wishing 'If only I hadn't said that!' At times we just don't understand why we behave the way we do. Life happens, one thing leads to another, and before we know it we've lost control of ourselves and the situation.

The words of Lao Tzu never fail to remind us of this:
Watch your thoughts for they become your words
Watch your words for they become actions
Watch your actions for they become habits
Watch your habits for they become your character
Watch your character for it becomes your destiny.

I have chosen the workplace as the context of this book, even though what you will read is equally applicable at home with our families. Why the workplace? Because that is where we spend most of our lives and generate the majority of our daily behaviours.

At the heart of the book is a powerful mind tool I have developed called The 5 Chairs which takes us on a transformational journey. Any reader who is interested in self-improvement will resonate with the contents of this book. Leaders and helping professionals will find guidance and support. Every page is inspired by an ambitious desire: that we all commit to bringing the very best of ourselves into the world in a much more conscious way.

The story behind the book

Over the past thirty years I have had the immense fortune to benefit from the life-changing lessons of some exceptional teachers, both in the business world and the spiritual world. I would not have written this book without the inspiration of three extraordinary individuals; the Vietnamese Buddhist Monk, Thich Nhat Hanh, the late Marshall Rosenberg, creator of the Non-Violent Communication approach and Eckhart Tolle, the German spiritual author and teacher, to all three of whom I dedicate this book. From my late twenties onwards, their combined wisdom and life teachings provided me with the inspiration I needed to sustain my own personal evolution. They helped me identify, understand and transform the dysfunctional behaviours which were preventing me from fulfilling my true potential in my own life.

After thirty years of working as a trainer, coach and facilitator in organizations and academic institutions, my hope is that this book will in some way help you on your own journey towards personal transformation and life fulfilment. I deeply believe in the ability we all have to constantly grow and evolve because we choose to do so. I am also profoundly aware of the perseverance and dedication required to achieve this. The 5 Chairs is designed to support you on this journey.

The Challenge

The challenge ahead of us is to:
  a)   better understand and master our own behaviours
  b)   better explain and manage other people's behaviours.

This doesn't come easily when people are pushing our buttons, especially at home when we're out of the public eye! In addition, we humans have a natural predisposition towards the negative. Just count how many judgmental thoughts go through your mind in a day and observe how the mind loves to focus on imperfections and problems.

We need to set ourselves a clear intention <u>to become exemplary in our behaviours</u>. We will fail many times, but if we learn to constantly question ourselves – 'Was my behaviour effective?' 'How could I have behaved differently?' 'What impact am I having?' – and if we give attention to this intention, things will change and our tendencies to 'misbehave' will diminish.

Why should we bother?

Let's step back and think about our everyday reality. Take a few minutes to ponder the following questions.

REALITY CHECK - **At work**

1. How many hours per day do you spend at work, on average?
2. How many years of your life will you spend at work?
3. How many waking hours per day do you spend with your family?
4. How do you usually feel when you get home after a day at work?

Broad answers:

1. It depends on where you are in the world but usually around 8 – 10, so about 80% of the day.
2. 45? The best years of our lives between 20 and 65.
3. If you're working full-time, 2-3 hours. Plus weekends of course, if it's not spent recovering from the week's work!
4. Only you can answer that. How often do you return home on your best form?

These answers are sobering. Most of our lives are spent at work rather than at home with our loved ones. Life at work can be tricky. Things don't always go our way. Our relationships can be difficult and we're certainly not always on our best behaviour. Survey after survey shows that 70% of the workforce is not happy with their lot.

We are in a constant emotional loop between work and home. We create moods and atmospheres which are contagious. If we argue with our family before going to work and then dump our grumpiness on our colleagues, it effects our office environment. Then if we're negative and hostile during the day we risk punishing our families when we return home.

Isn't it vital, therefore, that we invest time making sure we give the best of ourselves wherever we are? Shouldn't we all be helping to make the organizations we work for healthy and rewarding places to be in? Isn't this the responsibility of every single one of us?

Viktor Frankl in his book 'Man's Search for Meaning' said:

'Everything can be taken from man but one thing: the last of human freedoms - to choose one's attitude in any given set of circumstances.'

This book is about that choice. To choose an attitude in life which consciously contributes to the happiness and success of everyone, both at work and at home. This is our call to action.

Preparing the terrain

Be your own expert
So where do we start? In the words of Sun Tzu, 'Know thyself and know thy enemy!' When we fully understand the dynamics behind our unproductive behaviours they will begin to lose their power and we can transform them. The alternative? They will continue to run our lives and create frustration, depression and general havoc.

The foundation
Here's a question for you. Do you know *why* we judge each other, blame each other, gossip about each other, become defensive, complain and procrastinate? Do you know why we want to be right most of the time or have the last word? If a child asked you, 'Why do people do these things?' do you have an explanation at the ready?
We have to become experts in understanding and managing our behaviours. That's the first step.

A promise to you
I promise you that by the end of this book you will be your own expert in human behaviour and that you'll be able to:

    a)   better understand and master your own behaviours
    b)   better explain and manage other people's behaviours.

You will have the awareness and skill to modify behaviours which are not serving you well and you will develop a repertoire of behavioural change strategies that will ensure you attract success into your life.

To make this happen, we need to embrace two fundamental beliefs:
Belief 1: *We are responsible for all our behaviours*
This especially includes the bad ones! Whenever we misbehave in the moment we must agree to take responsibility and intervene with strategies such as a) forgiving ourselves b) saying we're sorry *c)* quickly choosing another more effective behaviour and moving on. No more blaming others. If we can choose our attitude in any given set of circumstances let's commit to taking full ownership of our behaviours.

Belief 2: *We can change*
How many times have you heard people say, 'That's just the way I am. I can't change!'? If you believe this, stop reading now. This book is not for you. We are changing all the time. We are learning new things all the time. That's why we're here. Nothing is set in stone. If we want to improve our lot and feel good about ourselves, we need to believe we can retrain our minds to change our habits.

The method
With these beliefs guiding us, we can begin consciously to distinguish between our productive and unproductive behaviours, to understand their dynamics and, where

necessary, intervene to transform them. I designed The 5 Chairs to help you do this. Over the past ten years I have used this mind tool with thousands of people of all ages and from all walks of life. It works well.

What is The 5 Chairs?

It's a *mind tool* and a *learning experience*. It consists of 5 chairs which act as a behavioural compass for us, mirroring our daily reactions and forcing us to track what we're thinking, what we're feeling and how we're behaving in any given moment.

It's a *game-changer* which encourages us to make new choices about what behaviours are appropriate to adopt in different circumstances.

It's a *change-accelerator* because the more we practise with The 5 Chairs, the quicker we learn to take control over our negative impulses and to adopt more positive behaviours to feel better about ourselves.

How does it work?
There are 5 different chairs which form the basis of this mind tool. They are:

1.   The Attack Chair
2.   The Self-Doubt Chair
3.   The Wait Chair
4.   The Detect Chair
5.   The Connect Chair

Each of the five chairs represents a set of attitudes and behaviours with a specific way of reacting to life. For example, when we're in the first chair, The Attack Chair, we judge, criticise, blame, shame, complain, deny, dominate and procrastinate, to name but a few! Behaving from this chair has consequences in the world which are mostly negative. If we become aware of this we can switch chairs and adopt a different approach to life. If not, we will continue to 'infect' our lives and the world with their negative energy.

The 5 Chairs is a bit like playing 'behavioural musical chairs', only the chairs don't physically disappear, instead their 'music' changes. As we move through our daily lives we can choose which chair to sit in when we're conscious. If we're uncomfortable we can move chairs. Often, however, we become hostage to a chair and unknowingly get stuck in it.

When I run live workshops, the five chairs are the protagonists, lined up centre-stage in front of the participants. They are our point of reference. We use them to examine our behaviours in depth. Participants sit in them, speak from them, question them, move them and learn from them.

In the following chapters we will explore each chair and its behaviours in depth. We will identify the values and beliefs running the chairs, the language and behaviour we produce from them, the attitudes which most characterise them and the core lessons we need to learn from them.

In any one day we might find ourselves sitting in all of the chairs at different times either consciously, by instinct or by default. The chairs nudge us into self-reflection and self-awareness. They force us to question what impact our behaviours are having. This requires a high level of vigilance on our part, a real challenge if you consider how distracted and cluttered our minds are today. So to ensure our success, I added another metaphor to anchor our practice.

Each chair comes with an *animal metaphor* which acts as a type of early warning system for us. Our brains love simple language and react well to strong images and associations.

The animals are:
1.   The Jackal
2.   The Hedgehog
3.   The Meerkat
4.   The Dolphin
5.   The Giraffe

What immediately comes to mind when you think of each of these animals? What associations do they activate in you? My hope is that they playfully activate a sort of self-detection mode in you. Sometimes it's easier to recognise ourselves better in other beings!

The reason for choosing these particular animals will become clearer in the following chapters but I trust you have already drawn your own conclusions.

The book and the programme
This book is the fruit of The 5 Chairs transformational programme which I have run and tested with thousands of participants over recent years. The core mission of the programme is to help us retrain our behavioural patterns in a highly experiential and practical way using real life situations and challenges. For anyone interested in following the programme, the book is essential foundational reading.

The 5 Chairs programme develops **Four Core Practices**:
1. Self-awareness
2. Self-mastery
3. Understanding other people
4. Managing our relationships

As we slowly gain a clearer perspective of the dynamics of human behaviour by practising on ourselves and with others, we begin to access a fuller spectrum of harmonising behaviours.

The Key Questions
To help us achieve this heightened awareness, we need to constantly ask ourselves the following questions. Try and imprint them on your mind and return to them as often as possible.

What impact am I having on the people and the environment around me?
Are my behaviours serving me well?
Am I in control of my emotions or are they controlling me?
How am I leading myself in every moment and my relationships?
Am I holding difficult conversations or avoiding them?
Am I expressing my full potential?
What are people saying about me when I'm not with them?

Our behaviour is the foundation of our productivity, our creativity, our confidence and our connection with others. It's worth doing the work.

What do I ask of you as you read?
To benefit from The 5 Chairs process, I invite you to be *courageous, patient and disciplined.*
Courageous enough to step back, examine and question the daily behaviours and attitudes which are not serving you well.
Patient enough to accept that learning new behaviours is a process which takes time, so try not to be too hard on yourselves.
Disciplined enough to do the exercises suggested in the book, over and over again, until you have adopted your new desired behaviours.

Outcomes
If you apply yourself to this journey, I guarantee you will improve the quality of your lives. Your relationships will become more supportive and collaborative and you will enjoy deeper levels of satisfaction and fulfillment in life. The better we feel about ourselves, the more generous and understanding we are towards others.

Our behaviour is the foundation of our productivity, our creativity, our confidence & our connection with others. It's worth doing the work.

CHAPTER ONE
What World Are We Living In?

It's worth spending a few words to contemplate the world we're living in, as our behaviours are directly affected by our context. Our lives are unfolding against the backdrop of the often quoted 'VUCA' world, a world where Volatility, Uncertainty, Complexity and Ambiguity are centre-stage. The speed of change around us is overwhelming. No sooner does someone declare 'it can't be done' than someone else is already doing it. The digital world whisks us along from one life event to another at great speed. Expectations are high. Competition is fierce. Time is scarce.

How do we find the appropriate strategies to successfully manage this reality and still remain relatively positive, stable and open to each other? Very often we don't.

A client of mine called me with the following cry for help.
'We're having problems in our team. We're constantly bickering with each other. Our meetings are inconclusive and unmanageable. Nobody listens anymore. Everyone thinks they're right! Operations and Sales are at each other's throats. Productivity is down and staff morale is at an all time low. We just can't afford to go on like this.'

How often do teams in organisations across the world face dilemmas like this? Take a group of people, ask them to work together and watch what happens. A myriad of human behaviours will emerge. We set out with positive intentions, eager to work and succeed together and then, as we grow more familiar with one another and drop our masks, our more destructive tendencies creep in as we start judging, blaming, complaining and gossiping. These behaviours are as irresistible to us as they are toxic.

If you think about it, most of us come into adult life poorly equipped with the collaborative skills necessary to create flourishing work environments. Despite our best intentions we often end up misbehaving with one another and damaging our relationships in some way. Our education system still fails to recognize personal growth and self-management as fundamental skills for the primary curriculum, so we stumble through our early relationships using trial and error and waste many of our most formative years just surviving in our co-existence rather than flourishing from it.

We have false expectations of our contract with life. We believe things should go our way. Nobody warns us that people will constantly disappoint us, disagree with us and frustrate us and that we will do the same back. We learn painfully that not everybody likes us or wants to be with us, and that this is just the way things are.

Trigger happy
We are all walking triggers. Moving bundles of emotions. What we do, what we say, how we say it, how we look, how we talk, even the way we eat, constantly triggers reactions in people around us, whether positive, neutral or negative. It might be a word, a phrase, a facial expression, a tone of voice, an attitude or an event. We cannot NOT have an influence on the world around us. Even when in isolation we are constantly influencing ourselves!

Most days we will find ourselves in three recurring trigger situations:
1. We will trigger other people with our own behaviour.
2. Other people will trigger us with their behaviour.
3. We will witness other people triggering each other.

We can take an active role and intervene assertively in each of these situations or we can hide away and succumb. That's our choice and that choice will directly affect the success of all our daily relationships.

Let's run through an example of what happens in The 5 Chairs when we're triggered by someone else's attitude or behaviour.

A 5 Chair simulation
Imagine you're in a meeting. You're explaining an idea you've worked on for a new project when one of your colleagues, Johan, interrupts you with:
> *'That's a crazy idea! It'll never work.'*

This is a provocation. All eyes are on you now. How will you react? Below are five different reactions from The 5 Chairs. In each Chair we look at 1) what we might be thinking about the provocation and 2) what we might say. We then examine the behaviours and attitude driving our reaction.

In The Attack Chair
We think:
'What a cheek! Who the hell does he think he is. The idiot!'

We might say:
'You always do that. You always butt in and invalidate people's ideas before they've even had a chance to finish talking. Can't you just listen for once!'

Behaviour:
Our tone of voice is aggressive and accusatory. Non-verbally we're sending eyeball missiles to him as we boil inside.

Attitude:
In this chair we immediately interpret the trigger phrase as a personal attack and match it with a counterattack. We load our verbal guns and fire. This person needs to be put in their place. Our ego needs protecting and defending. We feel indignant and outraged and show it!

In The Self-Doubt Chair
We think:
'I suppose he's right. Another dumb idea of mine! I always stick my foot in it. I should have just kept my mouth shut. I don't know why they assigned me to this project in the first place.'

We might say:
'Yes, I suppose you're right. You usually are. It's a crazy idea.'

Behaviour:
In this chair we become self-conscious. We've been attacked so we curl up in defence. We withdraw from the rest of the meeting with a massive sulk all over our body, self-esteem shattered, self-confidence at an all time low. We start engineering an excuse not to attend the next meeting.

Attitude:
We reject ourselves and cave in to the belief that we're just not intelligent or worthy enough of respect or consideration from others. We feel powerless and weak. We self-sabotage.

In The Wait Chair
We think:
'Stay calm now. Don't take it personally. I don't want to over-react. I might regret it later. Stop. Think. Breathe. Count to 10! Let's examine the situation from all angles.'

We choose NOT to react. NOT to speak. We manage ourselves.

Behaviour:
We slow down. We pause. We observe. We suspend judgment. We take a deep breath, steady our bodies and minds and try to source our inner stability. We're on sentinel duty. Very attentive. Looking out for potential self-sabotage. Preparing ourselves for the appropriate next move.

Attitude:
We're in the chair of choice. We know if we respond from the Attack or Self-Doubt chairs we will either damage the relationship or self-sabotage. We decide not to take things personally. We work on staying in control of ourselves and the situation. Our goal is to be effective not reactive.

In The Detect Chair
We think:
'Wow. He just cut me off. That's really irritating. I'd like to be able to openly contribute my ideas without having them dismissed. I'm open to disagreement but I'd appreciate some sort of respect first and also some rational explanation or clarity.'

We might say:
'I can see you don't agree with me and I'm curious to understand why, but before doing that can I first finish explaining my idea?

Behaviour:
We are calm and assertive. There is no aggression or punishment in our voice.

We remain emotionally steady and we speak our minds clearly and respectfully. We are transparent about how we're feeling and we tend to our needs. We request collaboration from the other person.

Attitude:
We get in touch with the feelings arising in us as we hear our colleague's words and we recognize our need for respect, recognition and contribution. We focus on getting our needs met in the moment. We're using our powers of observation and we're thinking objectively and strategically rather than emotionally. We speak up in a respectful way.

In The Connect Chair
We think:
'That was a brusque reply. He seems visibly irritated at what I said. I wonder what triggered that response in him? He seems very convinced about something. I'm curious to know why he reacted like that.'

We might say:
'I obviously said something which is not in line with your thinking? I'm curious to know what's on your mind. What is it about my idea that doesn't work for you?'

Behaviour:
In this chair we show authentic curiosity. We switch our attention away from ourselves and onto the other person. We look beyond their emotions, their judgment and criticism and try to understand what needs they might have which are not being met.

Attitude:
Our intention is to connect rather than correct. Our desire is to stay in the conversation despite the emotions. We are curious about, not judgmental of, the other person's reaction. We empathize with them and proactively seek to understand what they need. Our leading question is 'What's important for them right now?' Our final objective is to get both our own and the other person's needs met in collaborative understanding.

Reflection
Without knowing the full context of the situation, which of the above reactions would you most likely have had?

What impact would each of these reactions have had on the other people present?

How would each reaction have affected the rest of the meeting?

As I previously mentioned, each chair is a world unto itself with recognisable thinking patterns, attitudes and behaviours. We are constantly moving from one chair to another during the day. Life in The Attack Chair is very familiar to us but it usually generates suffering. In The Self-Doubt Chair we tend to feel uncomfortable with ourselves and hide from life. If our emotions are running high, we skip The Wait Chair. The Detect Chair invites us to speak our truth and be fully accountable in our own lives and The Connect Chair inspires us to deeply connect with others.

We all experience different levels of comfort in each of these chairs and we all have our favourites.

The work with The 5 Chairs is designed to create a shift in us. As we become more aware of our moment-to-moment reactions to life, new choices open up to us about how to interact with one another. As we move from Chair 1 to Chair 5 we embark on a journey of transformation from:
     judgment to empathy
     resistance to acceptance
     victim to player
     semi-sleep state to real awareness
     separation to connection
     unconscious behaviour to conscious behaviour
     'what is' to 'what could be'

In the coming chapters we will explore each chair in depth. But before we do so I need to tell you more about two of the fundamental players, the Jackal and the Giraffe.

CHAPTER TWO
Spotting The Jackal and The Giraffe

Some years ago I attended a powerful nine-day course of Non-Violent Communication in the presence of its late founder Marshall Rosenberg, a man whose contribution to world peace has been monumental. That course changed my life. It deeply influenced my way of feeling, thinking and communicating in the world. I was also introduced to two very powerful metaphors created by Marshall Rosenberg himself, which I constantly use in The 5 Chairs programme. They are 'the Jackal' and 'the Giraffe'.

The Jackal and the Giraffe are simple but powerful metaphors, in the form of hand puppets. These puppets serve to remind us of the quality of thoughts we are producing in any moment.

Think of a Jackal. What comes to mind? A small, cunning, opportunistic scavenger that fiercely defends its territory from intruders. Then think of a Giraffe. What do you envisage? A tall, graceful, noble soul, protector of the Savannah and keeper of the biggest heart of all land animals.

The Jackal represents our more judgmental thoughts and hostile behaviours whilst the Giraffe represents our more understanding behaviours which generate harmony and well-being. Which animal, in your opinion, is more dominant in our world?

Over to you
I have an exercise for you to bring this alive. You're going on a Jackal hunt to observe some of your Jackal behaviours in action. If you are a fast-forwarder, don't skip this part! It's crucial.

Challenge 1: The Jackal Hunt exercise
Turn to page 127 follow the instructions and come back with your findings. If you want to do this exercise with your colleagues or teams, download copies in The Academy section at www.the5chairs.com. Happy hunting!

So, what were your findings? How many ticks did you give yourself? How many other unproductive thoughts did you manage to produce?

Despair not. We all do it. It's human nature. Eckhart Tolle observes in his book 'The Power of Now', that

> *'about 80% to 90% of most people's thinking is not only repetitive and useless,*
> *but because of its dysfunctional and often negative nature, much of it is also*
> *harmful.'*

You might find this somewhat extreme but if we take a good look at the way we think most of the time, his observations are fairly realistic.

I now have another challenge for you.

Challenge 2: The Jackal Hunt continues

Return to your workplace and this time, instead of observing yourself, observe your colleagues. Your next meeting would provide a superb hunting ground.

As you participate, turn up the observer button in you. Scan the words, the thoughts, the behaviours, and the attitudes of your colleagues as they contribute. Don't forget to watch out for the more silent surreptitious Jackal behaviours too. The sneaky non-verbal ones such as the odd smirk, frown, raised eyebrow, sigh or head-shake. If you are courageous and resilient, extend this exercise to a whole day at work.

TIP: Other fertile terrains could be the coffee machine, your lunch break, your performance review, a meeting with your boss. In fact, any normal workday activity will do.

So what did you discover? Have you given up on the human race? Were you horrified by the Jackals you found rampaging through your organisation? Or were you already quite conscious of this ubiquitous human condition?

Next challenge.

Challenge 3: Giraffe Spotting

Let's now turn our attention to the the Giraffe. Please go to page 128 or go to www.the5chairs.com. Read the instructions and return to the savannah!

So, how many Giraffes did you encounter? How did you feel in the presence of Giraffe behaviours? What percentage of Giraffe thinking and behaving can you personally sustain during a whole day at work? How often do the Jackals sneak in when you're off guard?

Deep down we all know negative thinking is unproductive, exhausting and energy-sapping and yet it prevails in our organisations. Individually we all have a role to play in reducing this negativity.

If we are what we think, if our behaviours are the products of our thinking and if the quality of those behaviours impacts our destiny, isn't it imperative that we take a closer look at what thoughts we are manufacturing every day and what impact they are having on the way we live, love, relate, work, lead and parent?

The Jackal and Giraffe serve to remind us of the quality of thoughts, attitudes and behaviours we are producing in real time, what we are contributing to life and what impact it is having. These two puppets are always present at our live programmes. They prevent us from slipping back into our unconscious negative behaviours. They playfully keep us alert and nudge us into fuller consciousness.

The Ultimate Antidote to Jackal Thinking

To help you practise reducing your Jackal thinking, I have a powerful experiment for you. I invite you to go on a 'Mental Diet'. Turn to page 129. This is not for the faint-hearted. It will be one of the hardest things you have ever done in your entire life but is an excellent foundation for all the work we will do with The 5 Chairs, and if you achieve it, your life will change radically!

The Worlds of The 5 Chairs

We are now ready to explore The 5 Chairs in greater depth. The following five chapters are dedicated to an in-depth exploration of the behaviours and characteristics of each chair and the impact they have on our lives as we react from them.

CHAPTER THREE
CHAIR 1 – THE ATTACK CHAIR – The Jackal

'Never criticise a man until you've walked a mile in his moccasins'
American Indian Proverb

In this chair we judge, criticise, label, blame and gossip to name but a few. We're in the world of the Jackal. We focus on what's 'wrong' with other people and situations rather than what's 'right' with them. This is the entry point of most of the suffering we create in our lives. It's where we're 'out of' our minds.

This is the red chair, the Jackal chair. The chair of adrenalin and instinctual survival. It is forceful and persistent and commands attention. Of all the chairs, The Attack Chair is the easiest for us to identify with and recite from. We are very well versed in its language and can effortlessly reproduce its behaviours. Its voice can be theatrical and emotional or deadly silent and insidious. It easily consumes us. This is undoubtedly the chair which needs the most remedial work if we are intent on building a better world where organisations and families can thrive.

So what behaviours do we commonly bring into our workplace and homes from this chair?

Jackal Behaviours in The Attack Chair

Jackal behaviours are generally negative, uncivil, unproductive, hostile and aggressive and bring toxicity into our workplaces and homes. The list is long and we indulge in many of them on a regular basis!

blaming, finger-pointing	procrastinating
judging and criticising others	violating expectations
always thinking you are right	escalating
taking things personally	missing deadlines
gossip mongering	silo-ism
punishing others	dismissing other people's contributions
creating conflict	avoiding accountability
arguing	denying responsibility
taking revenge	being unreliable
complaining	manipulating people and situations
bullying	being opportunistic
intimidating colleagues	misinterpreting, misevaluating, mistrusting
invalidating others	imposing egos
discriminating against an individual or group	using abusive language
hoarding information or being secret	practising poor correspondence etiquette
ignoring people and problems	using 'power over' leadership

Any of these familiar? Of course. It's the way we've been programmed to think and react from an early age. It's what we've learned from our parents, schools, communities and society at large. It's our social conditioning.

But are we aware of *how regularly* we indulge in these behaviours, *where* they stem from and *why* we do them?

Core Beliefs in The Attack Chair

Many of these behaviours stem from negative beliefs we have developed from our experience of the world over time, such as:

'The world is a dangerous place'
'It's an unfair place'
'I need to be strong'
'I need to protect and defend myself'
'I can't trust people'
'People will want to take advantage of me'
'I need to be cautious'

When we judge others it is usually from a place of insecurity and fear within us. We often choose to judge people who are 'worse off' than we are which gives us an illusory sense of superiority and feeds our needy egos. Often our intention in The Attack Chair is to take control, to prove we are right and to display our power 'over' others. From an early age we are taught to see things in polarised terms of black and white, good and bad, intelligent and stupid, especially if we're living in more competitive domination cultures. This vision then translates into a 'you' versus 'me' mentality rather than a 'we' mindset. This usually results in estrangement, separation and conflict.

To counter Attack behaviours we need to be very vigilant about the thoughts and language we are 'manufacturing' everyday.

Jackal Thoughts and Language

Here are some examples of typical 'Attack' language you might come across in the corridors at work.

- Who did this?!
- You can say what you want. In the end I decide.
- It's urgent!
- Its not my job!
- They're idiots!
- Why didn't you …?
- It's not our fault. They ...
- It's got nothing to do with me.
- I sent you an email!
- It's impossible!
- He deserves it.
- You wouldn't understand.
- You're not paid to ask questions or give opinions.
- I'm your boss. Just do it!
- We've always done it this way.
- I told you!
- Have you heard the latest about...? (gossip)

How often do you hear or say similar things?

Negative Thought Management

Just how conscious are we of our negative thoughts? Most of the time they're on the rampage without us even knowing. And if we are aware of them, what should we do with them?

Should we:
  a. *Try stopping them by suppressing them?* 'I must stop thinking like this!!' Warning! That doesn't solve the problem at source and the thoughts will be back to haunt us.
  b. *Ignore them?* Warning! Same as above.
  c. *Obsess with them?* If we fan their flames and constantly mull over them, they'll take over and ruin our health and sanity.
  d. *Observe them?* Step back and witness them from a detached perspective? Take a good look at them, explore them closely and try to understand what's triggering them? Value them as our teachers. As an opportunity to learn?

The last option is obviously the best plan. But how often do we manage to do it?

One way we can begin to manage our negative thoughts is by **consciously cleaning up our daily language**.

The Power of Words

Words are powerful. Choosing the right ones in conversation is an art form. The words we choose reflect the intentions we hold. If there is incongruity between the two, we're in trouble. People can't read our minds, so paying attention to the words we use is vital, but not common practice.

Take for example a simple sentence with the verb 'to be' + an adjective, such as 'the British are unfriendly'. The literal meaning of this phrase is that ALL British people are unfriendly. A condemnation of an entire nation! This is obviously inaccurate. A more realistic description might be 'British people tend to show their feelings less on first meeting than other cultures'. More accurate. And yet, even the use of 'less' begs the comparison, 'less' than who?

How often do we risk offending each other with judgmental-sounding language? A declaration such as, 'He talks too much' rather arrogantly suggests that the person speaking knows exactly what is the acceptable amount of talking to do. But what if your 'normal' is not the same as my 'normal'. Who's right?

So how can we clean up our language and communicate more accurately with one another?

We can begin with Jidda Krishnamurti's belief that 'observing without evaluating is the highest form of human intelligence'. This is extremely challenging for us. I invite you to try it right now.

Look at the list of judgments below and transform them into simple factual descriptions of observable behaviour where there is no trace of personal interpretation or evaluation. Here are a couple of examples for you. The judgments are underlined.

Judgment: He's an <u>incompetent supervisor</u>.
Description: He doesn't carry out the duties that are expected of him as a supervisor.

Judgment: He's got <u>no sense of humour</u>.
Description: He didn't laugh at my joke.

Try transforming these judgments into pure descriptions without looking at the answers below:
Judgments and Evaluations
    a)   She completely ignored me in the meeting.
    b)   The deliveries are always late.
    c)   He's an idiot!
    d)   They never listen to us.
    e)   My boss just doesn't care.
    f)   They're inconsiderate.
    g)   He doesn't like me.
    h)   She's selfish.
    i)   You're totally irresponsible.

Descriptions and Observations
    a)   She didn't ask for my opinion in the meeting.
    b)   The deliveries didn't arrive on time four times this month.
    c)   He didn't follow my instructions.
    d)   We explained the procedure to them on three separate occasions but they didn't implement it.
    e)   I haven't received any feedback from my boss since the last performance review seven months ago.
    f)   They asked me to work on Sunday.
    g)   He didn't invite me to lunch.
    h)   She takes care of her needs but she doesn't take care of others.
    i)   This is the fourth time you've failed to inform Operations about the changes you agreed to with the client.

What impact does the quality of these two styles of language have on you? How do they both affect your thinking and feeling about the other person or the situation?

When we use factual rather than judgmental descriptions of people and situations, our perception of reality becomes more accurate. This is useful because we can radically reduce:
a) the risk of misinterpreting and misevaluating what we are experiencing

b) the likelihood of other people becoming hurt and defensive at our judgments
This practice of describing 'the' facts, and not 'our' facts is at the centre of any conflict resolution process. However it requires great vigilance. We are very quick to lapse back into judgments and evaluations. We've had years of training in it!

'Clean Up' Practice
Here is an exercise to help you become more vigilant about the language you are producing in daily situations and to help you translate other people's attack language into neutral statements.

* Start by listening carefully to the quality of language that surrounds you in your office and at home.
* Identify all the judgmental language you or other people produce.
* As you notice it, whisper to yourself, 'That was a Jackal!'
* Then practise translating the judgmental phrases you hear into 'neutral' observation language (it's good to take notes here to embed the practice).
* Watch the impact on your emotional state as you neutralise the language.
* Practise neutralising judgmental language in real time with yourself and other people. Translate sentences into factual, observable descriptions or ask questions to neutralise the other person's judgments.
  For example, for 'They're inconsiderate,' ask 'What exactly have they done to make you think that?'

The Impact of The Attack Chair on the Receiver
How does it feel to be on the receiving end of Attack Chair behaviours in the workplace? What are our common reactions?
• frustration, irritation, anger, fear, hurt, confusion
• withdrawal and avoidance
• loss of temper
• resentment
• diminished goodwill
• counter attack - verbal and non-verbal
• threats and warnings
• escalating to management
• complaints
• sabotage
• desire to leave

At an organisational level, the higher the level of toxic behaviours we generate, the lower the level of productivity and the greater likelihood of poor morale. Entropy increases stress, causes higher employee turnover and results in poor company performance, none of which is good either for human well-being or business results.

The Deeper Why
So WHY do we regularly display these kinds of unproductive behaviours, knowing how detrimental they can be to our well-being? Let's explore the mind mechanisms

behind some of our more insidious thinking and behaving.

In this section we will examine how our more toxic thought processes and behaviours negatively impact our relationships. Our minds are very cunning. If we're not alert, we are easily drawn into what I like to think of as 'Mind Games'. Below is a is a selection of some of the most common, which when in full flow cause havoc in our workplaces and at home.

a) The Storyboard Game

Our minds are never still. Thoughts stream relentlessly through our heads. On average we produce 70,000 thoughts per day, which makes 3000 per hour and 50 per minute. This is our monkey mind.

Watch your mind closely and notice how much it constantly comments on life. We are telling ourselves stories about reality all the time. We create a storyboard which becomes the backing track to all our life events and activities. Our mind even chatters in the background when we are talking directly to another person. It seems to have a life of its own. Fifty to eighty percent of the day our mind is in this state. Watch your mind when you're doing a simple task like peeling a potato. Where does it wander off to?

Let's see this in action. Imagine you've just arrived at the airport. You have an early morning flight to catch for an important job interview programmed for late afternoon. Just a one-hour flight, so plenty of time. You check the departures board. Flight cancelled. Bad weather at destination. Where does your mind go?

Storyboard 1:

We start commenting on the situation in our minds and build some negative stories about the incompetency of the airport services. 'Can't they even deal with a bit of snow! This is the twenty-first century, for heaven's sake!' and 'Why does this always happen to me!!' A justifiable distortion of the truth considering the situation.

As we get more upset and impatient we begin to complain out loud to gain support from others around us. 'This is just not good enough.' Other people agree with us. That makes us right. So now we're on a roll, feeding off the nodding heads around us. We choose to ignore the simple facts and get drawn into our own drama as the story spins further. 'They'll pay for this. I could lose a precious business opportunity because of their incompetency. I want to speak to someone in charge here. Now!'

Then, to prolong the suffering, we phone a friend or two, and repeat the story, adding a little more spice and indignation each time, feeding off their sympathy and confirming that life is just not fair. We are now extremely stressed out.

Reflection: If we run this narrative through our minds, the only thing we've actually achieved is to wind ourselves up, become miserable and be totally ineffectual.

Storyboard 2: The Alternative

After entertaining some Jackal thoughts about the situation, like 'Damn it!' or 'Rats!' which serve to momentarily voice our annoyance, we choose to see reality as it is, do some fact-finding, evaluate all our options and move into action. If there is nothing we can do, we accept the situation, immediately inform the company at destination and trust they will understand the situation. After all, it's out of our control. We then continue to live life pleasantly.

Reflection: If we run this narrative it keeps us emotionally stable, fundamentally optimistic and effective in the present moment. We experience relatively little stress and accept reality as it is.

Two very different mind scenarios. And who is responsible for the outcomes? We are, of course. The choice is always ours. If we all fall victim to this constant mind narrative the question we might need to ask ourselves is how can we transform it into something more positive, more productive?

Constant negative commenting on life rarely gets us anywhere. Have you ever come out of a meeting that went extremely well and noticed how quiet the mind becomes? Of course. It has very little to comment on! Compare that to an unsuccessful meeting. Our minds immediately begin to elaborate, comment and tell stories and we're sucked out of the present.

So, can we learn to be aware of our constant commenting? Can we practise transforming our negative narrative into more neutral, less emotional narratives? Can we remember that it is not the situation which is the problem but the way we think about it?

This means seeing people and events as they are, not as we are. It means seeing life without adding any story to it.

'New Thinking' Practice 1 – Story Reduction.

As you move through your daily life:
1. Observe how your mind *comments on everything* around you.
2. Track what you *add to reality* in the way of evaluations, negative and positive. Observe how your mind transforms reality.
3. Remember: We *create our own suffering* by the thoughts we choose to entertain.
4. Consciously choose to stop commenting in certain situations. Move to focus mode. Accept reality as it is, evaluate your options and act *without telling yourself stories*.
5. Ask yourself: '*Where does fact end and story begin?*'
6. Return to pleasant living as fast as possible.

b) The Judging Game

Another favourite game of ours. Have you ever spent a day without entertaining a single negative thought or judgment? Then you're not human! We are judging people and situations all the time. Whenever we meet someone, whether we are aware of it or not, we are implicitly and automatically judging them in some way. As Carl Rogers observes:

> Our first reaction to most of the statements which we hear from other people is an immediate evaluation, or judgment, rather than an understanding of it.

In milliseconds, and with very little information at our disposition, we decide how we feel about a person or a situation along a continuum from:
• repulsion
• avoidance
• tolerance
• acceptance
• appreciation

So why do we judge?

When we judge others, we do not define them, we define ourselves because our judgments actually reveal our own soft-spots, weaknesses and insecurities. If we harshly judge others it's usually because we do the same to ourselves.

There is a very fine line between using good judgment and being judgmental. Negative judgment usually shuts us down and prevents us from understanding the full situation. Most of our judgments about people tend to be based on incomplete information. We think we know a lot more about people than we really do. I use a trick with myself here. Whenever I see myself moving into judgment I ask myself the question 'What do I REALLY know about this person?' That keeps my Jackals at bay and moves me into curiosity, a much healthier state of mind and a good antidote to judgment. It's difficult to judge when you're curious.

Our Biases
This section would not be complete without saying a few words about our biases. Our speedy classification of people and events is masterminded by our unconscious biases, those prejudices which we have formed over many years of life conditioning and which have been left unquestioned, mainly because they are unconscious.

Neuroscience informs us that as human beings we process up to as much as eleven million pieces of information from the world around us at any one time. This is overwhelming. In fact we can only consciously process forty pieces of this information at any time. The rest gets filed in our unconscious. It's only natural then that when we're processing all this information our brain selects quickly and simply and we end up broadly categorising the world into a) 'I like it', b) 'I don't like it' or c) 'I'm indifferent'. These quick judgments then translate into micro-behaviours, the little things we do and say on a daily basis in reaction to life events. These behaviours play an enormous role at home and at work. So often they are unconscious and detrimental.

Micro-behaviours
Let's look at some examples.

a) Imagine you're talking to someone but you're in a rush. You're becoming agitated because you're late and want to end the conversation but you don't want to appear rude by interrupting. You might glance at your watch or check your phone or wiggle around a bit on your seat hoping the person will pick up the signals, understand your situation and stop talking.

Warning: Watch-glancing and phone-checking are two of the most commonly used micro-behaviours today.

b) You're leading a meeting and you ask for everyone's opinion about an idea you've just proposed. As you scan the faces around the table you unconsciously give more attention to your selected 'favourites' in the team who think and behave like you and usually support your opinions. You skip over the others.

c) During a recruitment interview you instinctively feel attracted to a candidate who is very similar to you and reminds you of how you were at the beginning of your career, a sort of mini-you. You think they would fit well into your tribe so you soften the questions and make the interview easier for them.

These micro-behaviours come with risks. They usually convey the message of 'I'm distracted', or 'I'm not interested' and are easily open to misinterpretation. Whatever impact they have, whether desired or not, the relationship can be negatively effected. The same goes for playing to our favourites. This can alienate and demotivate other team members. Just the same way, choosing a 'mini-me' can result in an in-group mindset.

We need to adopt strategies to reduce these risks.
If we're torn between listening to someone and moving to the next event we must speak up:
> 'I hate to interrupt you but I've got another appointment and have to go. Can we catch up later?
> In a meeting we can self-check: 'Am I including everyone in this conversation/ decision? If not, who am I excluding and why?'
> In a recruitment interview we can ask: 'Am I favouring this talent because they are like me or because they are suitable for the job? '

Managing our Differences
Instinctively we prefer what is familiar and move away from what is different. This choice is often unconscious and comfortable. When we are babies it's natural for us to embrace diversity but as we become young adults, constantly exposed to a world full of prejudices, it is educated out of us. Now, more than ever, working in global businesses with global clients and multicultural workforces, accepting and leveraging

diversity is a skill we need to re-adopt.

To reduce the impact of our unconscious biases we need to a) clearly understand how we can benefit from diversity, especially in our workplaces and b) consciously decide to manage the challenges diversity brings with it. At an individual level it means becoming very vigilant about the biased statements we make: 'She wouldn't be suitable for the job. She's a young mother.' 'He's an engineer. He wouldn't understand.' 'They're too young for the task.' 'They're too old for the job.'

The more we become aware of our biases the more we can question their foundations.

Byron Katie's work into self-inquiry is very helpful for us here. She encourages us to ask ourselves the following questions whenever a judgmental thought comes into our minds:

Is it true? Is it always true? What would it be like if I didn't have the thought?

c) The Defence Game

On to our next game. Another area of our lives that causes us great suffering is our attachment to and defence of our opinions.

We all build our opinions in different ways. We might invest time forming them by reading, researching, debating and reflecting. Or we might hear something which appeals to us on the media or from friends, and decide to adopt it as our own, not because we have checked its validity, but because it suits our world view. Whatever way we choose to build our opinions, once they are formed we easily become very attached to them. They feed our sense of self, our sense of identity. They become our truth, and even at times, 'the' truth.

So what happens when another person comes along and dares to challenge this opinion we now so dearly hold? That person becomes our moral enemy and we are left with only one option, to make them wrong by forthrightly defending our position and counterattack with a 'Yes, but ...' statement. But what exactly are we defending?

If we look at it more closely, an opinion is actually just a group of abstract thoughts, 'thoughts with preferences', as Eckhart Tolle calls them. They are intangible and transitory. They enter our minds and then exit. And yet we attribute deep existential value to these bundles of thoughts. They become much more that just viewpoints and when they are challenged, then so is our identity.

Why is it so challenging for us to listen to someone else's bundle of thoughts without feeling that our very existence is being threatened?! Can we resist the temptation of over-identifying with our opinions no matter how much time we have invested in forming them, and remain open and curious to other groups of thoughts?

Our minds are very tricky. We are easily led into unconsciousness. If someone has more, knows more or can do more than us, our egos often feel threatened. We feel 'less' than the other person and our sense of self diminishes. To restore this, we need to criticise or belittle the other person to put us back on morally superior ground. This becomes exhausting in life.

One of the managers who attended The 5 Chairs programme left me with a memorable metaphor regarding his own judgmental thinking. He talked about how he would load his gun before going into meetings in preparation for the battle, ready to defend his ground and push his case. In a follow-up coaching session when we were discussing how things were going after working with The 5 Chairs he replied, with a smile on his face, 'I've hung up my gun.' Sometimes all it takes is a good dose of awareness. His meetings are more productive now.

'New Thinking' Practice 2 – Hold your Horses

Here's some food for thought for you. Whenever you notice you're getting heated around your opinions, remember:

- Opinions are bundles of thoughts with preferences.
- Thoughts are abstract. They come and go. They are not 'you'. They are not your identity. They are passing guests in your mind.
- As you build your opinions don't get over-attached to them. They are likely to change anyway.
- Recognise other peoples' bundles of thoughts as being exactly the same phenomenon.
- If you feel yourself becoming reactive or getting on your high horse, stop and ask 'What's important here? What's *really* important? What's my deeper intention? Am I wanting to be right (alienating) or am I building an exchange with this person (connecting)?
- Be open to exploring other people's thought bundles and share your own generously, without attachment. In this way, you will be able to listen better and enrich your own portfolio of ideas.
- If someone else is fiercely defending their own opinions, step back, recognise the mind phenomenon in action and reduce the temperature of the exchange by showing them your willingness to explore their point of view before expounding your own. Do not resist or defend. Remain curious.

d) The 'I'm Right' Game

And that leads us on to our next game: the 'I'm right' game.

My brother once gave me some feedback on my own 'I'm right' behaviour at a family gathering which I have never forgotten. My mother tends to exaggerate. She has a highly developed sense of abundance. At the gathering she was asked how many guests were attending. She replied 'Thirty'. Wrong! My role was to correct her with a 'you're doing it again!' tone of voice. 'No Ma, not thirty. ThirTEEN'.

On hearing this, my brother touched me lightly on the arm and gently whispered in my ear. 'It doesn't matter'. Without pause for thought, my inner Jackal was triggered. 'What does he mean "It doesn't matter". Of course it matters. She is wrong and needs to be corrected.' My brother continued. 'Do you want to be in a relationship with your mother or do you want to be right?' Silence. Perspective.

My need to be right was transforming me into a 'know-it-all' policewoman whose role was to ceremoniously seek out and eliminate my mother's errors. Very distracting, not very sensitive, and in this case, completely inappropriate. People seldom enjoy being pulled up and corrected in public.

In fact, everyone loses in the 'I'm Right' game because it generates guilt, shame and punishment.

That day my brother's little nudge stimulated a fundamental question in me which I constantly ask myself whenever I'm tempted onto my high horse:

'What is important here? What is really important here?'

It helps me 'sharp' focus on my intention in the situation rather than on what is right or wrong about it. In my mother's case it wasn't important how many people were at the party. It was important to be connected to her gratitude and sense of abundance. Our insistence on 'being right' very easily leads to alienation and disconnection from others.

So what happens when we find ourselves in a conversation where we know we are right but the other person is unwilling, for whatever reason, to acknowledge the 'evidence' of a situation and stonewalls us? A sense of injustice can quickly arise here and indignation is just around the corner. If we allow our emotions to take over we will be derailed from our objective and the exchange will quickly sour. In situations like these it is vital to take a deep breath, pause and ask ourselves, 'What is really important here?' The answer will guide us to decide whether to drop it, pursue it or take it up at a later date. But our overall objective should always be to stay out of our emotions and in clear thinking. The more important the situation, the more difficult this will be, of course.

Can we really prevent our emotions from sabotaging our effectiveness?

'New Thinking' Practice 3 – I am 'A' Right
The next time you find yourself wanting to 'be right' in a conversation ask yourself the following questions:
- Am I listening to the other person or preparing my defence?
- What is my real intention here?
- Do I want to be right or be in a relationship?
- What is really important here?
- What is motivating their behaviour?
- If I am right, how can I transmit that whilst also managing the other person's reaction?

e) The Blame Game

This is a big one! We all blame. No one is immune. It is a well-developed sport in the world of humans. As John G. Miller so accurately observed in his research on personal accountability, there is a cycle of 'blame-storming' in action every day that looks something like this: the CEO blames the vice president, who blames the manager, who blames the employee, who blames the customer, who blames the government, who blames the people, who blame the politicians, who blame the schools, who blame the parents, who blame their children, who blame their teachers and so on and so forth.

So what exactly does all this blaming actually accomplish?

I am a strong believer that the subject of blame should be addressed head-on in the workplace in an open and structured way. If not aired, it will go underground to fester and create enormous damage. And if not resolved it will quickly undermine both the relationships and practices of any organisation.

So, *naming and claiming* blame is the first step to reducing it.

When I work with clients where siloism is a central issue, I invite the key players of the team or organisation to do a 'Blame-Storming' Session that revolves around 7 key questions listed below. This forces people to analyse their blame dynamics in detail. The questions are designed to make us look at blame in a rational, objective way. Only by getting curious about what is destroying our potential effectiveness can we collectively work on identifying collaborative strategies to combat it.

After each question I have included a selection of answers gathered from participants who have attended The 5 Chairs programme. They are excellent at helping us navigate the muddy waters of blame.

Blame-Storming Questions
1. What is Blame?

Blame is a form of self-defence. It's a way of deflecting responsibility. It's a way of exposing other people's faults or failings. It's a form of intimidation. It's the accomplice of judgment. It's a way to punish others. It's the birthplace of shame. It's ingrained in us and it's contagious. It's a scapegoat. It's a behaviour we learn when we're young. It's a social disease. It's everywhere: at home, at work, on television, in politics, in education. It's easy to do. It's based on self-interest. It's inward-looking. It's painful and ineffective. It displays a lack of accountability.

2. Do we play the Blame Game in our organisation?

To date the answer to this question is a unanimous 'Yes'. People have also noted that the intensity of blame can vary depending on a) an organisation's tolerance of mistakes and b) the underlying value it gives to its people or c) the style of leadership adopted. It is clear that command and control leadership gives birth to blame whereas participative or servant style leadership aims to reduce it.

3. When and Who do we blame?

When do we blame? During change initiatives, mergers and acquisitions, reorganisations, lay-offs, economic down-turns, shortage of staff. When we're under pressure, make mistakes, risk failure or when we find ourselves in uncomfortable situations.

Who do we blame? Ourselves, individuals at all levels, management, team members, other Project or Cross-functional teams, other organisations, parts of matrix organisations – basically everyone in the Blame Cycle!

4. Why do we play the Blame Game?

To deflect problems away from ourselves. To escape responsibility for our actions. To look good, protect our image and get our way. To protect our ego.

5. Why do we try to avoid experiencing blame?

It's directly related to our image and reputation. We want people to think well of us. It's a universal need. Blame can reduce prospects of promotion and bonuses. Its consequences can range from mild embarrassment to deep shame, legal sanctions, loss of liberty and even, in extreme cases, of life.

6. What impact does blame have?

It invades and corrupts corporate cultures, weakening their foundations. It increases competition, erodes trust and undermines integrity. It creates fear and kills transparency. It stunts individual and organisational growth. It deflates morale. It creates internal tension. It harms client relationships. It blocks creativity and innovation. It reduces flexibility. It covers up errors and prevents improvement. It wastes money.

7. What can we all do to reduce our blame culture?

We can learn to take ownership for our mistakes and accept responsibility for our errors. We can see mistakes as a learning experience. We can create a 'safe' culture for making mistakes. We can analyse the root cause of the blame and use it as the basis for improvement within the organisation. We can underline the concept that 'we're all in this together'. We can change our blame questions to 'game' questions (see below). We can decide to be more personally accountable.

'New Thinking' Practice 4: From Blame to Game

Here is a very effective exercise to use with individuals and teams to reduce the blaming mindset. It involves learning to ask

'**Game**' Questions not '**Blame**' Questions

If we carefully observe ourselves when we are in blaming mode we do two distinct things.

    a)   We make judgmental statements – 'They're incompetent', 'That's totally unfeasible!'

    b)   We ask blame questions – 'Why are they always late?', 'What's wrong with those sales guys?'

In this exercise we're interested in tracking the blame questions we ask every day and turning them into more productive 'game' questions. For example, instead of asking:

When are they going to be more efficient? (blame question) we try asking:
How can we help them be more efficient? (game question)

Look at some examples of blame questions below:
'When are they going to give us more budget?'
'Why don't they improve their processes?'
'What's wrong with your supervisor?'
'When is somebody going to change that printer?'
'Who changed the draft?'
'Why can't they speed up production?'
'When is management going to talk to us?'
'Why do I always have to do everything around here?'

These are often the first things that come to mind when we're feeling frustrated or faced with a problem. Our reaction tends to be negative, defensive and blame-oriented. Notice that these questions begin with 'When', 'Why' and 'Who' and imply an element of complaining, blaming or procrastination.

What impact do these questions have?
'When' questions imply someone has procrastinated, wasted time, missed deadlines or worked poorly.
'Why' questions imply victim behaviour or some form of poor personal accountability.
'Who' questions imply the witch-hunt, seeking out the culprit.

What do these questions accomplish?
Nothing, except toxic reactions such as fear, incrimination, secrecy, withdrawal and defensiveness.

On one of his retreats, Eckhart Tolle gave a perfect example of the blameless behaviour of a friend of his. He recounted how he had borrowed his flatmate's car for the night and on returning parked it in the driveway but forgot to turn the car lights off. The following morning he found a note from his friend on the kitchen table that read, 'I found the car lights on. The battery is flat. Could you call this number for help?'

Not a trace of making the other person wrong. No blame, just observation and facts. The powerful difference between 'I found the lights on ...' and 'You left the lights on and now...'

What alternatives do we have to Blame Questions?
We can ask more productive questions. We can ask 'Game' questions where we choose to be 'in' the game of life, proactively contributing.

'Game' questions reflect that power of being in the arena of life.
- What can I do?
- How can I help?
- What can I contribute?
- How can I be more effective?
- What can I learn from this?
- How can I improve my performance?
- What action can I take?
- How can I make a difference here?
- How can I improve my performance?

All these questions begin with 'What' and 'How' and are self-referential with 'I' as the subject. They are proactive and empowering and launch us into action.

There is a difference in energy between 'Why don't the customers follow the regulations?' and 'What can I do to help the customers with the regulations?' We stimulate self-engagement, we rise to the challenge, we become players rather than victims. Blame is insidious and contagious if not blocked. It only takes two people blaming together to leak toxicity into the environment. Experiment with game questions, model them. Watch how the energy changes around you and how problems are more quickly resolved.
It is essential that we work as individuals to transform our blame cultures into game cultures. Asking 'Game' questions is one practical way to initiate this transformation.

f) The Complain Game - The Supreme Human Sport!
If the human sport of complaining should ever disappear, it would be a direct threat to the human race as we now know it! Complaining, along with blaming, is another of our most favourite sports. It's a form of socially gluing. It binds us together as a society.

Can you imagine not complaining about the weather? And what about politicians, taxes, poor service, the post office, public transport, traffic wardens, the educational system, ethnic minorities, the news, smoking, feeling tired, our love life, our children, our spouses, our parents, the neighbours, our bosses, our colleagues, pollution, no time, overtime, life ...! What would there be left to talk about?

This is what a World Class Complainer usually does:
1. Always exaggerate! All forms of embellishment are acceptable here. 'These foreigners are taking ALL the good jobs', 'It's IMPOSSIBLE to find good staff nowadays', 'They ALWAYS get it wrong', 'They took HOURS to serve me'.
2. Ignore the facts! The truth is totally irrelevant when it comes to effective complaining. It's essential that you ignore all the facts related to your complaint: in fact, make up whatever is necessary to support your case.
3. Always complain about things you cannot do anything about! You think people complain because they want to change things? Think again. Complaining is not about change. It's just about good old complaining.

4. Always compare the present with the past! Nothing is quite like it used to be, so capitalise on that. 'It wasn't like that in my time.' 'I remember when sales people were polite and kind.' 'What's wrong with young people today?' If you run out of things to complain about in the present, turn to the past. It's a treasure trove!

'New Thinking' Practice 5:
How do we combat this? For the sake of humanity, radically reverse the above rules and become a World Class Non-Complainer.

a) Be grateful, every minute, every hour, every day, for what you've got!
b) Always remember that our complaints describe what we don't want. Let's start talking about what we DO want, and formulate requests to ensure that happens.
c) Learn to be more assertive. Express your desires in a clear and respectful way. (Check out Chapter 6 about The Detect Chair).

Set up a complaint-free challenge in your company. The prize goes to the person who does not utter a word of complaint for the longest period of time. Everyone plays the role of monitor. Participants are elminated when 'That was a complaint' is declared.

g) The Gossip Game

Nobody's Friend
My name is Gossip.
I have no respect for justice.
I maim without killing.
I break hearts and ruin lives.
I am cunning and malicious and gather strength with age.
The more I am quoted the more I am believed.
My victims are helpless. They cannot protect themselves against me because I have no name and no face.
To track me down is impossible. The harder you try, the more elusive I become.
I am nobody's friend.
Once I tarnish a reputation, it is never the same.
I topple governments and wreck marriages.
I ruin careers and cause sleepless nights, heartaches and indigestion.
I make innocent people cry in their pillows.
Even my name hisses. I am called Gossip.
I make headlines and headaches.

Before you repeat a story, ask yourself:
Is it true?
Is it harmless?
Is it necessary?
If it isn't, don't repeat it.

Author Unknown

Gossip is common currency between us humans. It's an insidious social game which we effortlessly slip into. A research team from the University of Amsterdam discovered that up to 90 percent of total office talk qualifies as gossip.

Why do we indulge in gossiping?
We love knowing about other people's lives. In the USA celebrity gossip is a $3 billion industry. However, there is gossip and there is gossip. There is a difference between presenting people's lives based on the facts, as many biographies do well, and talking about them with disparaging remarks. There is a difference between work banter where reference to other people remains general, friendly and supportive and gossip, which directly attacks and undermines the likeability or credibility of another person.

It is essential for us to recognise when gossip is out of hand because if unaddressed it quickly leads to a culture of mistrust. It damages interpersonal relationships and reduces employee motivation and productivity.

What are the roots of gossiping and how to deal with it?
The first step is to know how to spot a gossiper.
A gossiper is fundamentally an attention-seeker and their art is 'character assassination'. They often speak with a low voice and use moralising undertones. They will give you more information than you care to know about. They have a me-versus-them mentality, love exaggeration and are usually suffering from a sense of insecurity.

The second step is to understand our intentions behind gossiping.
Are we gossiping because we want to feel superior? Is it because we want to feel more part of a group? Are we unhappy, envious or angry at a person? Do we want to be at the centre of attention (albeit temporarily) by sharing our gossip? How healthy are these intentions?

How will the gossiper be judged?
In some cases a gossip-monger can become a powerful point of reference for information gathering in companies. People want to know what is going on in their workplace, they want to discuss work issues. However, the validity of information offered through gossiping is questionable. Most of it is second hand, so how trustworthy is it?

'Who gossips to you will gossip of you'
A Turkish proverb

In most cases gossip-mongers are not particularly popular because they cannot be trusted. Spreading private information or negative judgments about others is generally a painful process when you're on the receiving end.

What options do we have if we find ourselves in situations where others initiate gossip?
    a)   *Join in.* Add your own. Increase the invective. Not generally recommended as it usually aggravates the issue further!

b)   *Walk away*. Decide consciously not to be part of it.
c)   *Speak up*. This is the most courageous action to take and the most effective. Staying silent condones the behaviour and gossiping about the gossiper just increases the gossiping!

What to do in practical terms? Here are some suggestions.
1.   If someone starts gossiping at work, model the behaviour you want to see. Express your discomfort at talking about someone who is not present to defend themselves:
     '*I feel uncomfortable talking about Jill when she's not here to defend herself.*' Then change the subject.
2.   Suggest that the perpetrator should directly address their victim:
     '*I think it would be better if you talked directly to John about this.*'
3.   Draw attention to the gossiping:
     '*I notice you talk a lot about Sally. Why does she interest you so much?*'
4.   Introduce the perspective of the other person and their needs
     '*Well, if we look at it from David's point of view, he probably ...*'

Gossip in teams
If you're a team leader it's essential to create a toxic-free culture. One toxic team member can destroy a team so assertive leadership is required to protect the team. If there are several gossipers in the team it's vital to address the issue with them directly, face-to-face, in a feedback/coaching session to help them understand a) the impact their habit is having and b) the consequences if their negative behaviour continues. It's also important to address the topic openly with the team at the outset, demonstrating the difference between positive gossip, where morale-building stories are shared and negative gossip, where working relations are destroyed.

What if someone says to you, 'Don't tell anyone will you?' or 'Can you keep a secret?'
Be aware of the trap. It is easy to be lured into secret-keeping when we're flattered by the trust another person shows us. It strokes our egos but it comes with a price. Your own honesty could be compromised at some stage. Be aware of the responsibility which comes with such a pact before you agree. If you feel uncomfortable with the situation, clarify your boundaries up front: 'I'd really like to support you but I'm not comfortable with keeping secrets.'

What options do we have when we feel the urge to gossip ourselves?
1.   Imagine the person who is the object of your gossiping can overhear you. How would they feel hearing your words?
2.   Check on the intention behind your desire to gossip. Is it healthy?
3.   Stick as much as possible to the facts rather than personal interpretations.
4.   Practise having difficult conversations with people. Build your courage and authenticity. Learn to say things directly to people rather than behind their back. This is a skill which we can all learn with careful preparation and using a diplomatic approach.

'New Thinking Practice 6'

Here is a Golden Rule for you when you're next tempted to gossip about someone:

> *ALWAYS assume that everything you say about another person can be*
> *OVERHEARD BY THEM.*

The Attack Chair – Conclusions

We have a lot of work to do in The Attack Chair if we want to create healthier workplaces. Often just the realisation of how things can be different and what alternatives are available to us can create a shift in us. I vividly remember the reaction of one female executive on The 5 Chairs programme who was, by nature, a strident, assertive and sometimes domineering lady. At the end of the first day of the programme I asked everyone to embark on a mini-mental diet and to consciously suspend judgment as much as possible until the following morning when we would reassemble. The next morning, she recounted her experience with shiny eyes.

Frequently overwhelmed by the VUCA world with a very heavy workload, she would return to her family in the evening and revert to her habitual mode of irritability, complaining and nit-picking with her husband and children, which often spiralled down into family squabbles with everyone going their separate ways or doing silent TV watching. But that evening she consciously changed her way of 'being' with her family, looking only for the positive aspects in everything that happened, even the rain! She created a mood of peace, calm and lightness in the house to such an extent that before retiring to bed her husband enquired after her tentatively, 'Are you ok, dear?'

She was amazed at how her vigil awareness had changed the whole family atmosphere that evening. By reducing her level of resistance and releasing her constant need for control, she also immediately felt lighter herself. She was profoundly moved by the realisation that she was the architect not only of her own happiness but of her family's too.

This is the power available to us every day.

Takeaways

So what are we taking away with us from The Attack Chair?

• The realisation that we all contribute to unproductive attitudes and behaviours in our workplaces and at home.

• That we all have the power to change this just by regulating our own unproductive behaviours in a more conscious way.

• That if a critical mass of people commit to doing this we can bring greater well-being and happiness into our lives both at work and at home.

The Challenge
Our daily challenge in this chair is: *How quickly can I turn my negative thinking around?*

To achieve this, I invite you to commit to practising the following six Jackal reduction practices outlined in this chapter and summarised below. Then watch the impact it has on reshaping all of your relationships.

Concentrate on *one practice per week for six weeks* and then repeat the cycle. Try also to do it collectively in your teams and families. Commit to banishing Jackal behaviours from your life, proactively! When you spot someone in Jackal mode give them a gentle nudge. 'That was a Jackal!'

The 7 Jackal Reduction practices

The Storyboard Game
Reduce negative commenting about life. Only work with simple facts and observations.
Don't over-elaborate reality.

The Judging Game
Always ask yourself before judging anyone or anything 'what do I really know about this person/this situation?'

The Defence Game
Always remember that opinions are just a bundle of abstract thoughts moving through your mind. Don't attach to them. I am not my opinion.

The 'Who's Right' Game
I am not right. I am 'a' right.

The Blame Game
Ask Game questions not Blame questions.

The Complain Game
Become a conscious world class non-complainer.

The Gossip Game
There are only two choices: walk away or speak up.

CHAPTER FOUR
CHAIR 2 – THE SELF-DOUBT CHAIR – The Hedgehog

The Self-Doubt Chair is arguably the most vulnerable of the five chairs. It solicits a host of different reactions. Some people are bemused by it, some scorn it, many tiptoe around it, those in self-denial reject it, 'I never sit there!', others, especially women, identify fully with it, 'I'm always in that chair!'

We know when we're in this chair because we feel vulnerable and our defences are up. We usually indulge in self-defeating behaviours by judging and criticising ourselves. We dwell on our defects and our unworthiness and chip away at our own self-esteem with negative self-talk. We're just 'not enough!' We give our power away to others or resort to victim strategies. We're hard on ourselves. In truth, we turn the Jackal on ourselves!

In this chair, our nudge metaphor is the Hedgehog. What's the first thing that comes to mind when you think of a hedgehog? Images of a tight prickly ball, an instinctive curl-up reaction to fear, a formidable shield of spiny defence protecting a soft vulnerable belly, a fearful expression in hiding?
Unlike The Attack Chair, where we can enjoy marvelling at our collective buffoonery, The Self-Doubt Chair is where we feel more self-conscious. It's the chair that needs the most self-compassion. Although we all have moments of self-doubt and self-blame, we're not always eager to admit to it, either to ourselves or to others. 'What would they think, if they knew?' Exposure is risky and shame, guilt and embarrassment are just around the corner, so best keep a low profile and hope nobody finds out. We wouldn't want anyone discovering our dirty linen, would we?

The Self-Doubt Chair: Thoughts and Language
In The Self-Doubt Chair we have a tendency to use a certain type of language. Here are some examples of typical self-blame thoughts and phrases. Observe closely and you'll notice that when we blame ourselves we use both 'I' and 'you' phrases.

'I' phrases
- I'll never be able to do that.
- I'm not intelligent/competent/beautiful/important/thin enough.
- It's all my fault.
- I don't deserve it.
- She's achieved so much. What have I done?
- Why can't I stand up for myself? I'm a failure.
- Why does it always happen to me?
- That's just the way I am. I can't change.
- They'll never choose me.
- I never have any luck.
- Nobody cares about me.

'You' phrases – but still referring to ourselves
- Why do you always get it wrong?
- Who do you think you are?

- You're so useless!
- You'll never be selected.
- You haven't done well enough.

Typical behaviours in The Self-Doubt Chair
Here are some recurrent behaviours that emerge when we're in The Self-Doubt Chair:

- denying responsibility
- staying silent
- playing the victim
- putting oneself down
- reduced engagement due to fear of failing
- avoiding challenges
- being passive
- whining, moaning and sulking
- showing extreme modesty
- resisting changes
- reduced collaboration

We've all experienced these behaviours. They interfere with our ability to be accountable to ourselves, our families, our teams and our organisations. They also prevent us from living our full potential in life. We all need to take a deep breath and examine them more closely.

Self-Reflection
Take a few minutes to ask yourself the following questions:

How aware are you of doubting or blaming yourself?
When do you doubt yourself most? At home, at work, at leisure, thinking of the past?
What is your self-doubt most directed at? Your abilities, your life roles, your appearance, your behaviours?
How do you behave when you're in self-doubt mode? Do you withdraw, shut down, cover up, become passive, become irritable, seek attention?
Can you recognise a pattern when you're in self-doubt?

In this chapter I would like to focus on three fundamental drivers that feed our self-doubt.

1. *Our Fears*
2. *Our Beliefs*
3. *Toxic Silence*

Understanding these driving forces is a step to improving our self-confidence in life.

Our Fears
In The Self-Doubt Chair we need to come to terms with our common fears. Everyone experiences fear in life but do we know what causes it?

Can you think of one fear in your life which has held you back from doing something? A fear that maybe stopped you from changing your job, giving someone negative feedback, leaving a dysfunctional relationship, asking for a salary rise, starting your own business, asking for more time for holidays?

Fifty different types of fear have been recognised in human behaviour. A Facebook survey involving a cross-section of around 170,000 people found that the biggest fears holding us all back are:

1. Fear of failure.
2. Fear of not being good or smart enough.
3. Fear of disappointing ourselves due to past mistakes.
4. Fear of disappointing others, in particular family, spouse, colleagues.
5. Fear of being rejected.
6. Fear of being blamed.
7. Fear of success. What if we then lose it or can't sustain it?
8. Fear of being ashamed, which is blame turned inwards.

All these fears fall into three main categories:
>our *Competence* – I'm not good enough
>our *Likeability* – People don't like me
>our *Significance* – I'm not worthy enough

When we don't recognise these as our fears we repeatedly fall back into our comfort zone and end up sabotaging ourselves.

The Fear Equation
Very often in life, facing our feelings and taking responsibility for our fears can be painful or daunting so it's easier to resort to other solutions such as food, alcohol, work, drugs, texting, internet, pornography. They fill the gap and help us numb ourselves.

There must be a healthier alternative!

Fear is an emotion that can paralyze us into avoiding doing what we need to do in order to reach our goals. I have my own story to tell here. I lost the copyright to a communication course I had written because I was afraid to stand up to the woman in charge of the project. I didn't want to rock the boat. I wanted to be liked so I failed to negotiate contractual terms which reflected my worth. The course was a huge success and was promoted across the whole of Europe but I failed to benefit financially from its success. In hindsight, I could see how my inability to confront her stemmed both from a fear of authority and an under-developed sense of self-esteem and self-worth. Even today when I recount the story, I still catch myself trying to rationalise my behaviour. 'There was nothing I could do. She and her husband were sharks. And anyway, they had never agreed to give copyright to anyone before.' Rational lies often help us justify our not taking action!

That was a lesson for me. It was a call to step up, but it was daunting. I didn't know where to start. My rational mind was telling me that I should stick up for myself but my emotional fear of authority and my 'I'm not enough' belief was keeping me small and acquiescent. It took a lot of conscious effort to reframe that fear. Assertiveness training or negotiation hadn't been part of my school curriculum, especially growing up in middle-class England.

My partner became the perfect mentor for me. Born and raised in Palestine, his negotiating skills were formidable. On our travels together throughout the Middle and Far East, he taught me the art of negotiating. He helped me retrain my brain around the whole concept of worth. Not just the worth of money, but also personal worth. I began with initial feeble attempts in bazaars, feeling embarrassed and uncomfortable at my new behaviour. After several attempts and excellent guidance, I slowly began to grow a new muscle. Instead of caving in at the first sign of resistance from shopkeepers, I learned to enjoy the local practice of challenging prices and standing steady. There is always a huge mark up on tourist goods in the Middle East and Asia and bargaining is expected by the locals. In Morocco there's a price for the Moroccans (low), a price for the French (middle) and a price for everyone else (high). This is valuable information to have at your fingertips as you enter any shop there.

The more I practised, the more skilled I became at bartering for a fair deal. Like so many skills in life, it takes conscious practice to make the shift. With each negotiation my confidence and ability increased. I was learning a skill that continues to serve me today in my career as an entrepreneur where I am called to defend the value of my work every day.

Sometimes when I look back on that incident in my life I wonder why I didn't just confront her. What is normal for me now wasn't in my repertoire then. Until I actually admitted I was afraid of her, something my ego wasn't too keen on doing, I couldn't turn it around. Facing our fears is the first big step to dissolving them.

What neuroscience is saying about fear

Today neuroscience has made giant steps in helping us understand the mechanisms driving our fears and how to release their hold over us. Brain science informs us that fear is, in fact, an unconscious biological response, based on a deeply rooted belief that something or someone can cause us physical, mental, spiritual or emotional harm.

When we sense fear, one of our automatic reactions is to move away from the danger, whether it's real or imagined. Many people don't hang around when they see a big black hairy spider on the wall. This happens in milliseconds and without any thought.

As soon as the fear circuit is activated in our brain, either from an external stimulus or an internal thought, the emotional response mechanism in our brain, produced by the amygdala, sends a lightning fast electrical signal which activates the right pre-frontal cortex of our brain. This is the default mechanism in our brain. What happens next is extremely interesting. That part of our brain projects into the future all the potential negative consequences that might happen to us (emotional or physical) and behaves as if it happening right now. It's designed to move us away from any real or potential danger and towards safety and comfort. As this happens, we experience symptoms such as feeling short of breath, our heart might start racing and then we start to tell ourselves some rational lies about why we shouldn't take action or move forward.

We all have individual fears, whether it be of failing, of flying, of falling, of spiders or snakes, of public speaking, of meeting new people, of taking risks. In order to manage these fears, we need to confront them with courage as they are rising. We need to remind ourselves that they are actually inbuilt protective mechanisms. Once we recognise them for what they really are, we can lower their threshold and move forward to meet our challenges.

A few words about our Self-Conscious Emotions

When was the last time you blushed, felt embarrassed or wanted to disappear under the carpet out of shame? These are our self-conscious emotions. They are very common in The Self-Doubt Chair. They are complex, and manifest primarily as **shame, guilt, pride, embarrassment** and **jealousy**. They usually arise in us when we feel we're not living up to our own internalised set of standards. These self-conscious emotions are the birthplace of our self-sabotaging behaviours. When we feel ashamed, for example, we shrink and withdraw from life. We lose our power. If we are consumed with jealousy, we look for strategies to punish our imagined offenders.

Every self-conscious emotion we experience has an impact on our natural behaviour. We move out of our comfort zone. It is therefore essential to begin to understand the root causes of these emotions because the more we understand the mechanisms that feed them, the better equipped we are to reduce their negative impact on ourselves and others.

Core Beliefs in The Self-Doubt Chair

Have you ever asked yourself why a three-ton adult matriarch elephant with a four-foot chain does not attempt to free itself from a wooden stake in the ground? As the biggest mammal on earth, which tears down trees with ease, its ability to do so is unquestionable. And yet, it does not. It makes no effort to break free. Its mind is captive to the conditioning it received as a baby when it was trained not to wander off. All those years later it still believes it has no power to escape the bondage.

We all have stakes and chains holding us hostage. Take a few minutes to contemplate the following questions.
  • Are you aware of the inner critic in you that is holding you back?

• Are you entertaining any beliefs that prevent you from doing certain things?
• What stories are you telling yourself which stop you from reaching your full potential?

Self-limiting Beliefs
Fears often stem from our young imprinting years when we find ourselves in an environment where we think we're not good enough or smart enough. We hold beliefs and perceptions about ourselves that cause us to feel disempowered, embarrassed or ashamed.

My Cambridge Days
I'd like to share one of my own stories to illustrate the power of how a self-limiting belief got the better of me. It was a belief which had a hold over me through my late teens and early twenties. The belief was 'I'm not intelligent enough!'

Being born and brought up in Cambridge, UK, you had to be intelligent otherwise you felt unworthy of the right of abode! That was my belief. I spent years trying to become 'intelligent' enough for the privilege. What mattered most in Cambridge was the quality of my brain. My heart, body and soul were optional. To become a fully-fledged Cambridge resident I had to display excellent brain power. Then, and only then, would I become a truly worthy citizen of the city!

The trouble all began during my last two years at high school when my brother was offered a place to study at Cambridge University. He WAS a worthy citizen! Up until then I had been a mere onlooker, venerating the top brains of Britain from a safe distance. Easy.

As I began to receive invitations from my brother's friends to frequent the inner chambers of the university, my self-limiting belief took hold.

Trepidation, fear and self-doubt would overcome me with every social invitation. How could I stuff my brain with the contents of the Encyclopedia Britannica in a week to be ready for that cocktail party on Friday? Panic. I'll be chatting with some of the top brains in Britain, if not the world. God! What if they talk about things I know nothing about? I must be able to converse intelligently about everything. Yes, everything.

And what if they use big words I don't understand? Well, just ask them what they mean, stupid! (Where did THAT voice come from?) You must be kidding! That's suicide! What if they ask my opinion and I don't have one? What if they discover I'm a fraud? Sure death. No, stop. Think. Reason. I need strategies. All intelligent people have strategies. They absolutely must not find out. Find out what? (There's that annoying voice again. Will you stop distracting me? I'm trying to practise being intelligent!)
Um ... I need strategies... I could always ask them questions. Yep. That'll work. Keep the attention off me and on them. Great.
One strategy won't be enough though. These people are super-clever. They'll see

through that one immediately. I need a repertoire. I could change the subject. Subtly, of course. Quote something from an interesting magazine I've read and manoeuvre them onto one of my favourite subjects. Yes. I can prepare all that in advance. Now I'm feeling confident. Wait ... I can't do that all evening! I need some exit strategies if the going gets tough. I suppose I could go to the toilet if the conversation goes way over my head. But then I risk spending my whole evening there! NOT a good idea. Maybe I should just stay at home and talk to the dog. No competition there!

Do you recognise any of this inner chatter?

My conditioning was deep and embedded. I was telling myself the story that, as we live in a competitive world where we are 'expected to achieve', if I didn't do so then I'd be a failure (not an option in my books then). Not only would I let myself down but also my family (not an option either!). I believed my value was extrinsically based on my external success rather than on my unique, intrinsic qualities.

When we get trapped in these narratives, life becomes a battle as we constantly attempt to fulfil external expectations. And when we fail to do so, we bring anxiety and suffering on ourselves. This is very common with high achievers and perfectionists who make unreasonable demands on themselves (and others) and then become highly critical of themselves (and others) when they do not succeed.

We all have self-limiting beliefs which prevent us from reaching our full potential in life. When these beliefs go unaddressed they can seriously impede our ability to grow and flourish.

Examining our beliefs

A dear counsellor friend of mine once asked me, 'Do you live in the real world, Louise?' At the time I didn't understand the meaning of the question, let alone how to answer it. 'Yes, I think so,' I flimsily stuttered. The ensuing conversation with her was enlightening. I have never forgotten it.

To my 'Yes, I think so,' she changed the subject and told me she was about to get married. This was real news to me! She had never mentioned anything about marriage up until then. She was triggering me on purpose to bring to the surface some of my fundamental beliefs about marriage. My unconscious thoughts, my emotions and my reactions to her news would reveal this to her.

'How fantastic. I'm so happy for you!' I instinctively replied.

That wasn't enough for her. She prompted me to go beyond my initial reaction and dig deeper. I was fascinated by what surfaced in me as a consequence. The following internal voices emerged.

'She'll have much less time for me. What about our girly evenings? I'm going to really miss them.'
'That's the end of our holidays together then!'
'Not sure she's marrying the right guy for her. It's a big risk.'
'Now I'll have to get used to including him in our social equation!'
'Marriage will probably be good for her.'

These spontaneously produced evaluations directly reflected my own personal beliefs about marriage, whether conscious or unconscious. They had been formed over time. Beliefs that marriage is all-consuming and endangers friendships, that marriage is risky because we are never sure if the person is 'right' for us, that marriage implies sacrifice and limits personal freedom, beliefs that despite all of this, marriage is good for us! Where did these beliefs come from?

Most of our beliefs are formed in two fundamental ways:

• We LEARN them from our parents and trusted carers BY EXAMPLE. My parents used to argue a lot when I was growing up so I presumed it was normal behaviour in a romantic relationship. They were, after all, my role models and so as soon as I started dating, I did the same. I ended up squandering a lot of relationships in the hope of finding someone who could match my arguing skills! When the relationships predictably ended, it was, of course, always their fault! After all, I believed that 'arguing is normal in a couple' and my parents are still together so it had to be true. I was living out my belief. It took me a string of broken relationships and lots of heartache and disappointment to realise that this belief was dysfunctional and not serving me well at all. My parents have been together for more than sixty-nine years. They have their own special magic. What works for them wasn't necessarily healthy for me. But because they had never stopped loving one other all those years, I naturally concluded that conflict was part and parcel of a successful loving relationship. It did, in fact, take a lot of self-reflection and the loving presence of my partner to help me unravel it all and build a newer, healthier belief, that 'you don't need to argue in a relationship to be happy!' How many beliefs go unchallenged in our lives?

• We are TAUGHT beliefs.
Growing up in England in the 60s we were taught that 'children are to be seen and not heard'.
Living in Italy, as I do now, children grow up with the opposite belief. Children are to be seen, heard and venerated! Could that be one of the reasons why it took me a good few years to find my voice and learn to speak up without being afraid of disturbing others? Many of our fundamental beliefs are based on the limited perception, reasoning and experience that we have as children. We can hold those beliefs for many years. They become frozen in us. Often we are not even aware of them and they are triggered over and over again, constantly influencing our behaviour.

What do we do with our unhelpful beliefs?

We need to recognise them, acknowledge them, question them and then release them.

The first step is to become aware of them. We can't change anything we're not aware of. We need to understand that our limiting beliefs are only the effects of our OWN conscious and unconscious self doubts, our fears of not being good enough, not being smart enough, liked enough or loved by other people. This is what creates that heavy sense of uncertainty in us.

We need to examine our associations with the things we fear by recognising the patterns that are keeping us stuck and then release them by reframing the meaning we give to them. It's about feeling the fear, seeing its story and acting in spite of it. When we notice that we're having a negative emotional reaction to a situation, we need to check how we are thinking about the situation.

We often over-react to situations and become upset without knowing why. For example, if our girlfriend or boyfriend is late for a date and we react in an overly emotional way, maybe we're not reacting so much to the lateness itself but to our belief that we are not being respected. These evaluations often happen automatically and are triggered by our deeper beliefs. The trick is to step in and ask ourselves:

'What does this situation mean to me?
What am I telling myself about this situation, this person?
Are there other possible explanations?'

This allows us to check whether we're being realistic or whether we're over-reacting. If we think we're being unrealistic we can attribute another meaning to the situation: they were late because of a problem at the office, bad traffic, they were distracted or stressed and lost track of time.
By exploring other possible explanations we give greater perspective to the situation. We shift the mind across different options which has an immediate impact of reducing the emotional intensity of the situation.

'People are not disturbed by things, but by the views which they take of them'
Epictetus (A.D. 50-135)

Reframing our thinking helps us retrain our beliefs.

TOXIC SILENCE - The Silent Voice

Another behaviour commonly displayed in The Self-Doubt Chair is silence. One of our greatest challenges in company life, and in life in general, is to find our voice and speak our truth.

How often do we refrain from speaking up even when we know we should? How often do we withhold our contribution and self-censor with our silence? When was the last time you wanted to say something but for some reason felt you couldn't and decided not to? How many times have you observed what could be done better in your workplace but haven't felt comfortable sharing those observations? What happens to these unspoken thoughts of ours?

What goes unsaid in a company is what hurts a company most. The 'what's left unsaid' usually results in accidents and mistakes, people disengaging from their commitments, dysfunctional communication between people and reduced collaboration. These are all extra costs to any company.

Extensive research has been carried out around this topic. A Gallup survey carried out on 1,000 employees revealed that on average:

85% of the employees feel unable to voice their concerns
70% hesitate to bring up their concerns and
42% admit to withholding information about routine problems at work.

The same survey also dramatically revealed that employees only directly intervene in about two out of five unsafe actions and conditions that they observe in the workplace. Critical examples of these behaviours were in hospitals where nurses would refuse to challenge surgeons when they were about to make serious mistakes, such as amputating the wrong leg of a patient, for fear of being ticked off and humiliated in front of everyone else. White coat authority was taking its toll.

What stops us from speaking up?
Some food for thought:
• Think back over the years and find an example of a major loss you experienced when you did not speak up.
• In examining your own personality and attitudes do you have a tendency to be silent in troubling situations or to speak up?
• Were you encouraged as a child to follow the belief that it is better to be seen rather than heard?'
• Do you believe the old saying, "Better to be quiet and thought a fool than to talk and be known as one."
• How often have you justified your silence with thoughts such as:
'It's his life. Let him make his own decisions.'
'She's old enough to make up her own mind.'
'I'm not his mother!'
'It's none of my business.'
'She knows the consequences of what she is doing.'

Why is it that so often we choose not to speak our minds?
There are two well-recognised causes for our silence:
1 Our old friend Fear and
2. A sense of Futility

1. FEAR - The dance of fear and silence

Fear is a big driver of unspoken thoughts. After years of dealing with this issue head on with programme participants, I have been able to identify, with their precious help, some of the most important fear-based dynamics which keep us from speaking up in the workplace.

These include self-preservation, hierarchy, hostility, risk of rejection, whistleblowing, childhood dynamics and company culture. I have dedicated a paragraph to each, with the hope that deepening our awareness of these dynamics will help reduce their hold over us.

Self-preservation
In every work relationship there is a dynamic of power at play which creates an element of inequality and vulnerability in the workforce. Someone else is paying us to reach results. Where is the incentive then to speak up and be disruptive? After all, we wouldn't want to bite the hand that feeds us, would we?

What stops us from sharing all those unexpressed ideas that could really improve organisational efficiency? An innate protective instinct in us tells us to play it safe. 'If I tell the director what customers are really saying about our services, my career will be over tomorrow, so I'd better keep quiet rather than deliver the bad news.' We use silence as a way to protect ourselves and to avoid confrontation. It's an excuse we use not to get involved or compromised.

Hierarchy
Just imagine as a young manager recommending or suggesting strategies for change to your boss in a meeting where senior leaders are present. Would that feel uncomfortable? How will they react? Will my boss resent me, a subordinate, bringing bright new ideas? Will he feel shown up or threatened? If so, how will his resentment impact me? If you're working under a command and control leadership style, the answer is obvious. Best be quiet.

Hostility
Sometimes we are afraid to speak up because in our past people in authority have been genuinely hostile to our suggestions. There are plenty of bullies in the workplace who display angry, abrasive and abusive behaviours. When we don't feel it's 'safe' to speak up, the status quo goes unchallenged. Our freedom to speak up relies greatly on the belief we are working in a culture free from bullying. Trust is essential for this sense of safety.

Risk of rejection
Fear of rejection or isolation is another strong driver of silence. What if I speak up in a forthright way. Will my colleagues see me as a threat to their safety? What if they feel disappointed or hurt? Will they then treat me differently or even look upon me as a fool? Will they distance themselves from me? That would be devastating. The fear

of 'being disliked' or 'being unpopular' is profoundly uncomfortable for us social beings. If people start avoiding or alienating us, that would be social suicide! The consequences are too painful for even the most resilient of us to endure. Best be quiet.

Whistleblowing
An implicit message floating down the corridor of many organisations is 'if you cross management and rock the boat, you're finished. So do as you are told, don't make any noise, deliver the targets or else.' People who are very career-focused are often quite happy to bury bad news. It takes courage and integrity to expose information or activities which are apparently illegal, dishonest, or incorrect.

Very often people prefer not to report problems, or if they do, they give up at an early stage through fear of endangering their jobs. If I follow my moral conscience and take action, will I risk legal action, criminal charges, social stigma, and termination from my position, office, or job? Personal risk is high and incentive low unless transparency is a well-embedded and protected practice in the organisation.

Childhood experiences
We bring our 'family' and our biography to work with us. Childhood experiences and beliefs can be very hard-wired in us and we carry them with us into adulthood. What if we were highly energetic when we were young, with a sense of adventure, even a bit disruptive or rebellious? And what if our behaviour was disapproved of by our caregivers and teachers? This can easily transform into the self-defeating, self-sabotaging beliefs, 'What I have to say isn't important,' 'My opinion doesn't count,' which we repeatedly act out by remaining quiet and small at meetings like 'good boys and girls'. We mistrust our own voice, recycle other people's opinions or defer to the 'experts' to gain acceptance and approval. We are constantly looking for strategies to hide our 'inadequacy'.

Company culture
Company culture plays a major role in employee silence. If the cultural norm of the organisation is characterised by strong supervisory control, ambiguous reporting structures, conflict suppression, poorly conducted performance reviews or even extreme politeness, people will stifle their concerns for fear of drawing too much attention to themselves or of rocking the boat.

Many organisations send out the message both verbally and non-verbally that quiet submission is the best way to keep your job or further your career. Speaking out is not always viewed as a courageous and praiseworthy act. Many people who publicly express their concerns about their companies are subsequently alienated.

2. FUTILITY
A second and even greater cause for not speaking up comes from a sense of futility. It's the feeling that even if I do speak up nothing will change. Here are some comments I have received from participants who reflected back this sort of hopelessness:

'My feedback won't get implemented so what's the use. Nothing's going to change anyway.'
'Nobody ever really listens to us. It's an uphill battle. In the end you just give up. What's the point?'
'They're not really interested in what we've got to say so I lose interest too.'

An additional reason why people feel it's futile to speak up comes from the belief that their bosses lack the power or influence to support them, or are risk adverse and just don't have enough character to stand up for them to effect the necessary changes. They don't feel represented.

In other cases, this sense of hopelessness derives from bosses not even wanting to hear suggestions for improvement either because they are happy with the status quo and are therefore not interested or are themselves overwhelmed.

And what if supervisors fail to address the real problems and just look for quick fixes? People then lose hope that the real issues will ever be addressed, let alone resolved, so they remain silent. This then leads to a host of further problems for the organisation and the problems behind the problems never get resolved.

> *'A person who asks a question is a fool for five minutes.*
> *A person who doesn't is a fool forever.'*
> Chinese proverb

What is the personal price for not speaking your mind and what are the personal risks when you do speak up?

The price we pay for not speaking up

What happens if we don't speak up? Where do our unspoken thoughts go? They usually simmer below the surface, fester and explode at a later date.
What if we work in an open space office next to a colleague who has a habit which irritates us and disturbs our concentration? What do we do? If we stay silent we might find ourselves slipping into passive-aggressive behaviours, surreptitiously punishing our colleague by cold-shouldering them or treating them with curtness or complaining about them to other colleagues. Is the problem resolved like this?

Seven good reasons why we should speak up
1. Our silence promotes our invisibility.
2. Our silence can be read as an active form of approval. If we disapprove and don't speak up people can accuse us of not making our stand, and then distrust us.
3. Our need to be comfortable can jeopardise our contribution to the greater good of others. We may be harming the very people we want to help.
4. Being active and vocal shows that we are committed. It brings our value centre stage.

5. We all have a unique perspective. If we wait around for people to read our mind we might end up
    a. Accepting tasks we don't have the time for or the ability to do
    b. Following projects we don't want, and
    c. Missing promotions we do want.
6. Our voice could become the courageous voice that encourages other people to come forward. This is an act of leadership and will be recognised as such.
7. The unpopular voice is often the game changer. Think of Abraham Lincoln, Martin Luther King Jr, Winston Churchill, Mother Teresa.

The personal risk
What could we be risking at a personal level if we speak up?

We could be met with resistance; (think again of Abraham Lincoln, Martin Luther King Jr, Winston Churchill, Mother Teresa).
We could be judged and labelled by others as being 'trouble-makers'.
We could be marginalised or avoided.
We could provoke undesired consequences such as bullying or retaliation.
We could be removed, especially if we're in a command and control style organisation.

Tanzan and Ekido
There is a splendid Zen story which perfectly illustrates the disruptive nature of not speaking up.

Tanzan and Ekido were travelling together on a pilgrimage. It was raining heavily and the streets were muddy. As the two monks neared a bend, they saw a beautiful young lady dressed in a silk kimono at the side of the road. She was standing there, staring forlornly at the road ahead, unable to cross. Without hesitation, one of the monks, Tanzan, lifted the young girl in his arms, carried her across the mud and put her down on the other side of the road.

His fellow monk, Ekido, looked on without commenting and the monks continued on their journey. At nightfall they reached a lodging place where they would spend the night and Ekido, unable to restrain himself any more, blurted out a reprimand, 'How could you, Tanzan! We are monks, sworn to purity! We do not go near women, especially beautiful young ones! It is highly risky for us monks! Why did you do that?'

'My friend,' replied Tanzan, 'I put that young lady down hours ago. Are you still carrying her?'
How many hours do we waste just ruminating or obsessing over ideas, problems, or concepts rather than just voicing our concerns? The end result is that, like Ekido, we become distracted by these thoughts and our attention is no longer on what we're doing in the present moment. We lose our effectiveness in real time.

What is the price of silence in an organisation?

When people withhold information, opinions, ideas and concerns, leaders have less access to what they need to improve the organisation. Silence shuts down the very creativity which is essential for innovation and change. It undermines productivity and directly effects the competitive advantage of the organisation. If organisations place too high a value on being polite and avoiding confrontation the culture of open feedback cannot thrive and the organisation's professional growth will be stunted. Unspoken thoughts are a loss to company intelligence and integrity.

Leadership has a fundamental role to play here. Only when a culture feels 'safe' will people dare to open up more. Only when people can make mistakes without fear of punishment will they take more risks. Trust is the antidote to fear. It is the role of the leaders to create this trust and then of every individual to protect it.

When is it important to speak up?

- When something is important for you.
- During brainstorming meetings. If you are not involved people might mistakenly perceive you as antisocial, apathetic or someone who has no ideas.
- When an assignment is not clear. Don't be afraid to ask for clarification. Not doing so could make you appear incompetent.
- When you are in pain. Whether you're experiencing migraine, backache or other pains tell your boss or supervisor or help others to do the same. If you judge yourself as being weak or a wimp because you need to take some time off you'll end up worsening your condition and hindering your performance.
- When gossip and rumours become damaging. When gossip is harmless you can easily ignore it and mind your own business. However, if it becomes toxic where, for example, you hear a rumour about someone which is not true, silence should be broken to maintain the integrity of the people and situations involved.
- Whenever you feel harassed. Harassment, whether emotional, racial, physical or sexual, disrupts work and can have a major psychological effect on us. It is essential to speak up with the person who is harassing and establish firm behavioural boundaries. Failure to do so will only worsen the situation.

When should we not speak up?

Although the advantages of speaking up outweigh those of not speaking up there are times when it would be wise not to speak up. These are the times when we are consumed by emotions and our capacity to think clearly and rationally is seriously impaired. This often results in passive-aggressive behaviours and the likelihood of our damaging relationships is accentuated. At such times we need to regain our emotional stability before speaking up.

Concluding Thoughts – The Self-Doubt Chair

All of us are acting from different levels of awareness in life depending on our individual personal development. We have one thing in common, however. In every moment we are doing our best. Even though at times our best is not enough for the moment at hand, blaming ourselves will not help. We are not perfect. We are on this earth to learn and to evolve. It's a process. If I don't think highly of myself, I can't expect anyone else to think it of me.

Can we learn to observe our self-sabotaging behaviours and agree that next time we will try to do better? No self-blame. Just self-compassion and a learning mindset? Can we learn to accept ourselves without waiting for someone else's approval? Can we stop trying to measure up to others and begin to enjoy our uniqueness?

> *'Nobody can make you feel inferior without your consent.'*
> Eleanor Roosevelt

Personally, whenever I catch myself in negative self-talk such as, 'I can't do this! I'm not competent enough,' I smile at my hedgehog voice, comfort it and switch to a question *'What do I need in order to achieve this?'* If I see myself as worthy and capable, I can achieve anything I set my mind to and my self-confidence will grow. Ultimately, how we see ourselves is much more important than how others see us.

The Self-Doubt Chair invites us to recognise the limiting beliefs and fears that are holding us back in life. When we begin to 'see' them rather than 'be' them, we can befriend them and release them. We are then free to be the person we need to be, to do what we are here to do, and to make our unique contribution to life.

CHAPTER FIVE
CHAIR 3 – THE WAIT CHAIR – The Meerkat

The Wait Chair is crucial. We're on the middle ground between The Attack Chair and The Connect Chair, the two extremes of The 5 Chairs journey. In this chair we wait before we react. We control our urges to act or speak impulsively. We stop and think, even if it's just for milliseconds.

The Wait Chair is fundamentally a silent chair. It's where the chattering mind is quietened. No words. No thoughts. Vigilant observation and deep listening comes forth here and radical curiosity takes over. It is the space between the world that triggers us and our chosen response to that world. It's where we manage our mind and guide ourselves to right action.

Our nudge metaphor in this chair is the Meerkat. If you are not familiar with this amazing rodent, I invite you to see some video clips of them on You Tube and marvel at their extraordinary powers of observation, stillness and concentration. I chose the Meerkat because of its exceptional sentinel behaviours. The Meerkat will stay on sentry duty for up to one hour at a time with unfaltering vigilance. That is exactly what we have to do with our own minds. Be on guard. On guard against the predator thoughts which can easily destabilise us.

Wait Chair Skills
To master The Wait Chair we need to explore our ability to:

a) **Choose our attitude**
b) **Cultivate presence**
c) **Develop inner stability**
d) **Choreograph our thoughts**

a) Choose our attitude
It is increasingly clear that one of the most fundamental skills we need to acquire in our workplaces today is the ability to manage and embrace the uncertainty of constant change. For many of us this is counter-intuitive. The volatility, uncertainty, complexity and ambiguity of the VUCA world is not welcoming. It usually causes us discomfort.

Can we learn to become comfortable with uncertainty? Can we accept unpredictability as a norm? Can we recognise that we are part of a dynamic system and learn to manage ourselves better in the face of change?

I would like to share a story with you which I feel displays the type of behaviour which can serve us well in times of uncertainty and change.

My Palestinian friend
In the summer of 1994 I worked in Palestine for two months as a voluntary teacher in a school near Jerusalem. It was at the end of the first Intifada and before leaving I had a goodbye meeting with a Palestinian friend. That meeting had a profound impact on me.

Every day, along with many other West Bank Palestinians, my friend had to pass through an Israeli checkpoint to reach his place of work. The crossing would be more or less pleasant depending on the soldiers on duty, but it was often a challenge. Checkpoints are places of high tension where emotions flare, tempers crack and violence is just around the corner.

On this particular morning he had an important interview to attend and needed to cross the checkpoint quickly. The day hadn't started well. He was already late owing to family concerns; his aging father was sick and his pregnant wife was not well.

On arrival at the checkpoint his impatience to pass quickly was noted by one of the soldiers, new to the watch. He explained his situation and pressed for fast passage. The soldier blocked him and told him to return home. There would be no passage for him that day. My friend explained his situation once more. It was vital he crossed over. Another firm no. He insisted once more, to which the soldier shouted. 'If you wanna cross over, you take your clothes off. All of them!'

I still remember my sense of disbelief on hearing this. I went straight into The Attack Chair as my indignation flared. I envisaged all the possible ensuing scenarios: his reaction, his resistance, the shouting, the scuffles, the fear, even gunshots.

'So what did you do?' I urged, awaiting confirmation of one my imagined scenarios. He looked at me with extreme calm. Not a trace of malice or revenge in his eyes. 'I said nothing,' he replied. 'I looked the soldier straight in the eye. Then I slowly undressed.'

I was humbled into silence. This is not the reply I expected. As he continued his story, things became much clearer to me. The choice he had made in that instant was guided by a profound awareness of self and other. On receiving the soldier's ultimatum, he breathed a deep conscious breath, looked the soldier in the eye and from a place of calm and stability within himself, made his choice not to engage in the drama of the situation. He remained totally focussed in the present moment and observed the simple facts of the situation. No commentary, no added story, no past, no future, no ego. Feelings of outrage or humiliation would have been perfectly justifiable in this situation, but he chose not to go there. Instead he focussed on what was important in that moment, what really mattered. His work and his family.

From there he calmly moved into action. He undressed slowly, folded his clothes in a pile, nodded at the soldier and crossed the border, his integrity immaculately in tact. His very presence and inner steadiness disarmed both the soldier and the situation.

I was deeply impressed by the quality of his thinking immediately after the soldier's provocation and quizzed, 'How did you do that? How did you manage to stay so calm?'

'Why react?' he answered. 'The soldiers are doing their jobs. They're trained to control us. Some of them are young. They can't take the pressure. They crack. An emotional reaction would have worsened the situation for me.' 'But the humiliation of it all ...' I suggested.

'Words can be weapons or just words. It depends what value you give them. Nobody can rob me of my dignity unless I decide to give them the power to do so,' was his reply. He achieved his objective and made it to the interview.

I often reflect on this situation in my quieter moments and realise again and again how critical clear thinking is for self-leadership, especially when the unexpected happens.

My friend's encounter is a great example of
    a) accepting whatever the present moment contains and working with it rather than resisting it
    b) thinking clearly under pressure.

'I'm at the checkpoint. I need to cross. The soldier has asked me to take my clothes off. If I don't do this, I won't cross today. It's important to cross. I'll undress.' No stories, no psychological baggage attached, no ranting about what's right or wrong. Just presence, clear thinking, wise judgment and right action. Fairly counter-intuitive for most of us humans and yet something worth aspiring to and practising.

The two months I spent in Palestine marked the beginning of an awakening consciousness in me.
Viktor Frankl's words in his book Man's Search for Meaning took on a deep meaning for me.

'Everything can be taken from a man but one thing: the last of human freedoms–to choose one's attitude in any given set of circumstances.'

This is a responsibility we all need to assume in life and not a day passes without my reminding myself of it.

b) Cultivating Presence
How can we source that inner calm and presence my friend displayed when we are constantly reacting from highly energised minds which are full of mental and environmental noise?

The corporate world is beginning to take meditation seriously. Articles such as 'CEOs who meditate', '14 Executives Who Swear By Meditation', 'Who says there's no time to meditate?' are more and more commonplace today and CEOs are openly sharing the benefits they reap from daily meditation practice.

Bill George, former CEO at Medtronic, who now teaches at Harvard Business School, says, "The very best time to meditate is on a plane. I have to go to Europe a lot. If I land at 8 a.m., meditation gives me an opportunity to get deep rest and refocus before my board meeting at 10." At Medtronic, George dedicated one of the firm's conference rooms to being a quiet space where employees could go for a break (Bloomberg News).

Legal Sea Foods CEO *Roger Berkowitz* told Inc. Magazine, "The first thing I do in the morning is retreat to my den and meditate. I meditate twice a day for twenty minutes, closing my eyes, clearing my mind, and repeating my mantra until I'm in a semiconscious state. Sometimes, I'm wrestling with an issue before meditation, and afterward the answer is suddenly clear."

Green Mountain Coffee Roaster founder *Robert Stiller* told Bloomberg News that he regularly brought in a meditation instructor to the company's Vermont-based offices to lead employees in meditation. "If you have a meditation practice, you can be much more effective in a meeting. Meditation helps develop your abilities to focus better and to accomplish your tasks."

Ray Dalio, founder and CEO of Bridgewater Associates, the world's largest hedge fund, has built many of the Transcendental Meditation principles into his firm's culture. Transcendental Meditation informed Dalio's 'belief that a person's main obstacle to improvement is his own fragile ego.' Prior to practising meditation, his leadership style was constant, unvarnished criticism of others. People would take it personally and no one would propose a good idea for fear of being wrong. He was closing the workforce down with his behaviour.

Why meditate?
Meditation brings many benefits. It refreshes us, brings us fully into the present moment, makes us wiser and gentler and helps us cope better with overwhelming circumstances. Most importantly it helps us make better decisions by resisting the urge to react from the Jackal Chair.

The ultimate goal of The Wait Chair is to create a conscious space between life's stimuli and our response to them. In his book The Seven Habits of Highly Effective People Steven Covey refers to this space as a giant pause button where we reflect before we chose our response.

The very nature of meditation helps us achieve this. But not immediately. Let me share from my own experience what a typical short meditation session can look like when we first start learning the practice of meditation.

The teacher
   Find a comfortable position to sit in with a straight back. Breathe in and out slowly, relaxing a little more with every out breath. Slowly let go of all your concerns. Empty your mind of thoughts. When you see them entering your mind, invite them to leave. Your body's feeling calm and you're at peace. Take another deep breath...

The beginner's mind
   Ahhh! This is feeling good. I'm enjoying this. At last some respite from the office. Breathe in. Breathe out. Breathe in. Breathe ... I wonder if the others have

got their eyes shut? Mustn't look. That's cheating. Concentrate. The teacher's just said invite your thoughts to leave. I like the idea of inviting my thoughts to do things. OK. Good. I haven't got any thoughts at the moment. Must be doing it right. It's not as difficult as I thought ... damn. My knee's itching. Can't scratch it. We're not supposed to move. Maybe if I breathe it will go away. I could do a quick scratch. Nobody would know. Can't concentrate with that itching going on ... God, I've just remembered. I haven't answered that email from my boss. He wanted it by 4 p.m. He'll kill me. Now what am I going to do? I just can't cope with everything right now, especially with Jane off ... Whoops, I'm supposed to be meditating, not thinking about work ... Breathe in, breathe out ...

Meditating gets us directly in touch with our wandering mind! When we're beginners we're plagued by distractions. To resist the urges requires deep focus. That's why meditation is excellent for us. It helps us resist those in-the-moment urges and gets us more focussed.

When someone makes a mistake at work and your urge is to yell at them, what other choices do you have? Or when you want to blurt something out in a meeting but know you'd do better listening. Or when you want to check your emails every three minutes instead of focusing on the task at hand.

Conscious Pausing
Creating small pockets of silence during the day is not that difficult. It just requires resolve. Two to five minutes of slow conscious breathing in silence can be very effective. Think of our workdays. One meeting after the other with little time even for a biological break in between. No time to digest or reflect on what was discussed in one meeting before the next is upon us. New information, new challenges, new decisions. By the end of the day, overwhelmed by layers of accumulated information, we have very little recollection of anything that was discussed.

Whenever I work with teams I always invite them to spend a couple of moments in silence at the beginning of our sessions to help them bring their whole selves into the space where we'll be working together.

People are not used to doing this in the corporate world. We're always 'on' and convinced that we don't have time to stop. When the teams I have worked with consciously take time for a pause before starting a new activity they invariably declare, 'What a relief just to stop for a moment!', 'At last some respite', as they allow themselves to just 'be' rather than 'do'. We are, after all, human-beings not human-doings. As people begin to feel the benefits of conscious pausing, they ask for more.

If you pay attention, you'll notice that many times a day we unconsciously drift off and lose our alertness. If you manage to catch yourself doing this, check where you've gone.

'Where am I? In the past? Or in the future?

We need to become expert at tracking our own thoughts because if we're caught up in the emotions of the past or future we're definitely not being effective in the present, where most of our challenges are. We need to keep returning to the here and now.

A Simple Practice

Conscious pausing is very simple. Sit on a chair (or a cushion on the floor) with your back straight so that your breathing is comfortable. Set a timer for however many minutes you want to pause. Once you start the timer, close your eyes, relax, and don't move, except to breathe, until the timer goes off.

Focus on your breath going in and out. Use the words 'in' and 'out' as you breath to help you focus. Every time you have a thought or an urge to take you away from 'in', 'out', notice it and bring yourself back to your breath. That's it. Simple but surprisingly challenging. The mind loves action. Try it today for five minutes. And then try it again tomorrow. And the day after until it becomes a practice. Do it several times a day and you will really begin to feel the benefit.

I recommend you do this before returning home to your family. We need to 'clock out of' the stress and tension of the workplace before we return home to make sure we offer the very best of ourselves to the people we most love. A manager friend of mine makes a conscious practice of sitting in his car for five minutes to detox before he joins his family for the evening. It's become his ritual.

Practising Presence:

- Practise five minutes of meditating with conscious breathing twice a day.
- Practise tracking your thoughts. When you see negativity arising in you, ask yourself, 'Where am I?' If you're negatively chewing over the past or anxiously launched into the future it will have an impact on how you're performing in the present. Notice this and bring yourself back to the here and now.
- Between one work event and another, take the time to honour yourself. Pause, breathe and become still. Centre yourself before you move on.
- Take a few minutes in your teams to 'decompress' in silence before beginning your meeting or activity.
- Take time to wind down after work before going home so that you don't 'dump' your stress and tension on to your family.

c) Developing our Inner Stability

An excerpt from Rudyard Kipling's poem '*If*' comes to mind.

If you can keep your head when all about you
Are losing theirs and blaming it on you,
If you can trust yourself when all men doubt you,
But make allowance for their doubting too...

This ability is more crucial than ever today. Leaders, in particular, need to cultivate this type of presence. Where to start?

Observing our emotions – the ninety-second lifespan of an emotion

The brain scientist Jill Bolte explains that an emotion such as anger lasts just ninety seconds from the moment it's triggered until it runs its course. Only one and a half minutes. This is good news. If we can just 'sit with' an emotion for ninety seconds it will naturally subside.

But what do we usually do? We make it last much longer. We fuel it with our repetitious thoughts, our stories and what should last just one and a half minutes gets drawn out for five minutes, half a day, one week, even years! Instead of letting emotions run their course, we stir them up. So, how can we counter this?

Whenever you feel triggered and an uneasy feeling comes up

WAIT FOR NINETY SECONDS!

Just be present with the sensation. Experience the emotion directly. Let the lions roar and stand steady as the heat passes across your face.

Multiple interpretations

Another way to dissolve our negative emotion is by using multiple interpretations.

I can decide to interpret a mistake as a) an opportunity, b) a disaster or c) a blessing. I can react to an invitation as a) an obligation, b) an opportunity or c) a pleasure.

If someone loses their temper with me I can a) think they're an idiot or b) imagine they're having a bad day or c) understand if I am partly the cause.

A shared reality can be interpreted in different ways. Just ask some friends about their impression of a film you have seen together and you'll receive a myriad of interpretations. But do we consider this when we're 'in' situations, especially when we're triggered? And how often do our first interpretations go unscrutinised?

The exercise of entertaining multiple interpretations has an immediate impact on us. We become curious and curiosity is the key driver in The Wait Chair. Curiosity dissolves negative emotions and radically improves our effectiveness in our daily affairs.

Multiple interpretation practice:

When you're next triggered try the following:

- Watch your negative emotions rising.
- Check the meaning we're attributing to the event that triggered the emotions.

- Distinguish between what is really happening (which often goes unclarified) and what your personal interpretation is.
- Ask yourself, what different interpretations can I find for this situation? Identify at least three.
- Allow the emotions to dissolve.

Watch our Challenge Moments

To add to this practice we can begin to measure our real steadiness in life by closely observing how we react to unexpected challenges that come our way, both big and small.

Watch yourself as challenges arise and ask:
    What throws me off balance?
    What creates negative reactions in me?
    When do I lose my patience?
    When do I lose my presence?
    What topics of conversation set me off?
    Who are the people that set me off?
    Where am I (in what location) most often when my triggers are set off?
    Who are the people I tend to avoid?

This is deep inner work. Keep a journal of your answers. Only by consciously understanding what triggers us can we work on building new strategies to transform our reactions. This requires close attention.

Life is a series of challenges. That is our everyday reality. Ekhart Tolle invites us to 'accept every moment as if we had chosen it. Work with it not against it. Make it our friend and ally not our enemy.' Rather than seeing our challenges as an annoyance or a disturbance, they become our potential teacher, an opportunity for us to evolve. This is an important mindshift for us.

So, can we learn not to complain when things go wrong? Can we practise welcoming these challenges rather than resisting them? Can we decide not to react negatively when our expectations are not met? This is our choice: to resist or align. Here is a simple practice to help us in our challenging moments:

1. **See a challenge**
2. **Accept it**
3. **Align with it**
4. **Meet it**

If we are open and curious to learn, all judgment falls away and our energy automatically lifts because the mind will not judge when it is curious. The Persian poet Rumi depicts this masterfully in his poem The Guest House.

> *This being human is a guest house. Every morning a new arrival.*
> *A joy, a depression, a meanness, some momentary awareness comes,*
> *as an unexpected visitor.*
> *Welcome and entertain them all!*
> *Even if they are a crowd of sorrows, who violently sweep your house*
> *empty of its furniture,*
> *still, treat each guest honourably.*
> *He may be clearing you out for some new delight.*
> *The dark thought, the shame, the malice. Meet them at the door*
> *laughing and invite them in.*
> *Be grateful for whatever comes because each has been sent as a guide*
> *from beyond.*

Can we practise this?

'Small Irritations' Practice
One excellent way to cultivate The Wait Chair skills is by learning to quickly manage life's daily irritations. It might be bad weather, getting stuck in traffic, train delays, a parking fine, our favourite cafe being closed, forgetting our umbrella.

These are minor annoyances in our lives but provide excellent training in moving quickly through our negative reactions into a place of acceptance of the here and now from where our 'best self' can respond to life. The more we learn to manage our small irritations, the better prepared we will be for greater adversity when it arrives.

d) Choreograph our Thoughts
I have designed a sequence called 'Thought Choreography' to help us practise managing our thoughts when we feel triggered by someone or something. The sequence is designed to keep us AWAKE, CONSCIOUS and PRESENT as negative thoughts enter our minds.

1. Life Event
Something happens to us in life. We are triggered. Notice how our body sensations change (tension, heat, contraction etc). Track the rising emotions (irritation, anger, embarrassment etc). Just observe them and stay present with the discomfort.

2. The Jackal Show
Now watch carefully as the Jackal thoughts build in your mind. Just observe them. Don't judge them. Just accept them. Give voice to them if necessary – e.g. 'Damn!' 'Hell!' 'What!?'
This will release your negative energy but be very vigilant. DO NOT feed them or dwell on them or they'll take over. Move on quickly.

3. Ninety seconds of presence
This is the turning point. TAKE A CONSCIOUS BREATH and access your

inner resources of stillness, presence and stability. Count ninety seconds and let your emotion run its course. If you don't have ninety seconds because you're mid-conversation do a condensed version and just breathe a conscious breathe. Come into focus.

4. Switch attention
Consciously switch attention away from the Jackal and Hedgehog Chairs. Staying in these chairs won't get you anywhere so MOVE.

5. The Welcome Committee
Welcome whatever life is offering you in the moment. ACCEPT it as if it were meant for you. Do not resist it. We are here to learn and evolve! Accept the challenge.

6. Curiosity
Become curious about your challenge. Get interested in what's happening. Really interested. Explore it from different angles. Don't judge, label or criticise. What can you learn here? EXPLORE.

7. My Best Self
Now ask yourself, how would my BEST SELF react in this situation? Study the options open to you. Practise some advanced perspective taking. Weigh up the benefits of all your options for yourself, for others, for the situation itself. Then choose.

8. Choose and Move
Check your choice is as 'right' and 'ecological' as possible for EVERYONE involved. Make your choice. Move into CONSCIOUS ACTION (which could also be non-action).

I designed this process to help us
a)   reduce the time we spend dwelling on stagnant judgment and
b)   move more quickly towards conscious action.

Practise it daily when you feel negatively triggered by someone or something. Check which step in the sequence challenges you most and practise that with more intentional focus.

Concluding Thoughts – The Wait Chair
When I ask people on my programme to choose the chair they would most like to master in the future, their choice is so often The Wait Chair. There is a deep understanding that the practice of 'waiting' or 'pausing' before reacting is essential in order to transition from the negative to the positive and from the unconscious to the conscious.
When we feel the urge to 'act out' in our normal default ways The Wait Chair invites us to stop and think, to sit in the middle ground and feel the full force of two extremes – right

and wrong, black and white, yes and no, true and false.

In this chair we experience the fundamental uncertainty and edginess of life and learn to sit with it without behaving in ways that are harmful to ourselves or to others. It's our opportunity to really contemplate how we're behaving in our lives; how we might be hurting ourselves and others; what old habits we need to shed that are no longer serving us. We come face to face with our old repetitive patterns, our old trigger behaviours and we have the chance to experiment with new ways of behaving.

The Wait Chair is our pivotal point. It represents the choice we are faced with daily as leaders, colleagues, spouses, partners, parents and friends. We can succumb to our old dysfunctional ways or choose new more positive behaviours. The choice is ours.

On a more personal note
I would like to deviate from the main text of the book and share with you part of my own inner journey which spearheaded the creation of The 5 Chairs programme and which has made me passionate about helping other people discover their own full potential. I also hope that it will encourage you to keep pursuing your own path of growth.

Until my early thirties my external confident veneer had been very effective at hiding what was a fairly disorderly and confused mind! I had various well-developed behaviours that I would have quite happily disowned such as jealously, stubbornness and self-doubt, but I had very little notion about where to start. Deep down I knew it was possible to feel differently. I had had glimpses of inner calm and longed for those moments to become more permanent. How to achieve that became my main purpose in life. I decided to 'work hard' on myself. I explored many approaches including Hatha Yoga, Mindfulness training, Neuro-Linguistic Programming, Meditation, Non-Violent Communication, Pranayama Breathing, Tai Chi, Inner Mirroring and more. I was addicted.

Every time I embarked upon a new teaching or practice I was freshly convinced that I had now found the way to greater happiness and well-being. This was usually followed by a gradual dropping off of enthusiasm, the setting in of disillusionment, a good bout of self-criticism and then despair. I did, however, occasionally allow myself the luxury of believing that all this effort was beginning to bear fruit. Change definitely was possible, with the right amount of patience. I knew that. Thirty years of mental imprinting does not transform overnight.

I'd like to share three practices with you that had a profound effect on me then and which I still return to everyday for guidance.

Practice One – Mind-watching
A pivotal moment in the taming of my own mind came during a one-week silent retreat in Colorado with the Vietnamese Buddhist monk, Thich Nhat Hanh. A liberating

experience for some, a nightmare for others. On arrival at the centre I was informed by one of his monks that I would be joined by another nine hundred people. My immediate reaction was to turn on my heels and head straight back to the airport. I'm glad I didn't. The impact of the retreat was truly profound. The mere experience of practicing mindfulness with nine hundred people in silence was, in itself, a revelation. I had no idea how pleasant and efficient human beings can become when they stop talking.

During the retreat we were constantly encouraged to become aware of our thoughts, feelings and actions and develop a state of vigilant observation. A bit like being your own watchdog or guardian angel. Hence the metaphor of the meerkat.

At the beginning I found it quite daunting to witness the endless activity of my own mind. If you take a minute and watch the voice in your own head you'll know what I mean. That constant and often involuntary flow of commenting, identifying, judging, complaining, comparing, craving, liking, disliking, controlling, blaming and desiring we met in the Jackal Chair. I watched my mind flick back to the past, project into the future and then return to the present with alarming speed. My 'monkey mind' as the Buddhists and Hinduists call it, was on the rampage. Swarms of psychological memories coming and going. Relentless chatter. I felt I was being swept along by a stream of superficial thoughts over which I had no control. Most disquieting.

Our challenge during the retreat was to quieten our mental noise and sink into 'noble' silence. This would help us get in touch with ourselves at a deeper level where we could meet and free ourselves of some of our more self-defeating habits. Just what I needed. The means was meditation. I practiced devotedly but was horrified to discover how competitive I would become with myself as I grappled with my own ego to achieve this mental silence! When I did finally achieve it, the very act of observing my own mind actually created the space I needed for more inner clarity and I slowly began to experience the deeper inner calm Thich Nhat Hanh alluded to.

We were practising mindfulness, which in essence means attending to what's happening to us internally and externally and being aware of the interaction between the two. To do this well requires presence, being in the here and now, which is difficult when you're mostly in the there and then, as I was.

As I continued practising I became acutely aware of how much resistance I had to cut through. It was exhausting. That got me thinking about the whole concept of acceptance.

Practice Two: Radical Acceptance
Marcus Aurelius said 2000 years ago:
> *'Accept whatever comes to you as woven into the pattern of your destiny,*
> *for what could more aptly fit your needs?'*

The act of accepting what life has to offer is something I try to practise daily. This does not mean becoming a doormat to life but rather it means staying proactively and consciously responsible for how we are responding to life rather than becoming a victim to it.

What do we do when we feel offended, annoyed, confused or frustrated by what someone else has or has not done, has or has not said? This is where mindfulness helps us to observe, witness and create that space between the stimulus and our response. That critical space where we are free to make a choice.

I gradually discovered that only in that pause, however momentary, can we discern the most effective way to proceed. Any suffering we are experiencing ceases to be suffering as soon as we form a clear and precise picture of it. What we then say or do is much more likely to be an effective expression of our real selves coming from a deeper level of creativity rather than an automatic emotional response.

I have found this practice of acceptance and suspension of judgment of vital importance to me in my profession as an intercultural trainer. As Robert Kegan, the developmental psychologist, so succinctly said, "to function successfully in a society with diverse values, traditions and life styles requires us *to have a relationship to our own reactions rather than to be captive of them.*"

It is that ability to resist our tendencies to make 'right' or 'true' everything which is familiar to us and 'wrong' or 'false' everything which is strange. This brings me onto my last practice.

Practice Three: Choice.
This was, and still is, the most significant practice for me.

The realization that I always have a choice in life was profoundly liberating for me. Previously I would find myself being drawn along other people's decision-paths, both consciously and unconsciously. My need to please people radically disempowered me and my voice would often be stifled and lost.

The realisation that I alone am responsible for my well-being and that I can always choose what attitude to have towards life in any moment, was a turning point for me. It created a deep flow of energy in me. Knowing that I can always choose with intention and never have to default to being a victim was immensely empowering.

When faced with a situation, difficult or otherwise, I know I have options which I can consciously choose from. I can intentionally take action, deal with a situation and change it. I can accept the situation as it is, (being careful there is no residual resistance). Or I can postpone my reaction to a later time when I am more ready. I have that choice. Always. And the consequences of my choices are my response-ability.

These practices have brought me much greater inner stability. The work was worth it.

CHAPTER SIX
CHAIR 4 – THE DETECT CHAIR – The Dolphin

The Detect Chair is blue, which in Buddhist philosophy is the colour of a pure and uncluttered mind. I named this chair 'Detect' because it invites us to evolve from the 'little me' of The Self-Doubt Chair and step up to the 'higher me' where we can begin to make a difference, both in our own world and in the world at large.

In this chair we develop SELF-AWARENESS, practise SELF-MASTERY and aspire to authentic SELF-EXPRESSION.
Our guiding belief in this chair is: 'I know enough and I am enough.'

Our nudge metaphor in The Detect Chair is the much beloved Dolphin. Apart from being playful, self-assured, communicative, exuberant, fearless and extremely social, the dolphin is one of the very few mammals that displays self-awareness by responding to itself in a mirror. It also displays a high level of intelligence and collaborative problem-solving skills. It is the ideal metaphor for our journey towards self-realisation.

The Detect Chair invites us to do many things. We become more self-aware. We learn a new language, a language of empowerment in which we can confidently express our emotions and communicate our needs in an assertive way. We learn about the power of being vulnerable and the art of leading difficult conversations. We learn to step up into our full power.

Self-awareness is the most important building block for any personal growth and the only way to achieve self-awareness is through self-reflection. This means having the willingness to step back and take a good look at ourselves, which can be scary. It's much easier to blame the rest of the world for our pain rather than take personal responsibility for it.

In The Detect Chair we learn to reconnect with our emotions.
  'We are not thinking machines. We are feeling machines who think.'

This quote from an article by Richard Restak, Professor of Neurology at George Washington Hospital University School of Medicine and Health, puts our emotions clearly into perspective and reminds us of their importance. Our emotions, unlike our thoughts, are universal. They transcend culture, race, social class and age and they define our similarity as human beings. And yet for the most part we are either disconnected from them, controlling them or hiding them.

The Brazilian Emoticons
A Brazilian client had a powerful story to tell about how his factory workers found an effective way to manage their emotions and keep emotional outbursts in their workplace at a minimum.

Every morning the workers adopted a routine of silently declaring their emotional state to one another. As they entered the factory they posted one of three emoticons next to their names on a billboard - a smiley face, a miserable face or a neutral face. When I enquired how this ritual had helped them, they replied that by asking themselves, 'How am I feeling today?' they became much more aware of what they were bringing into the workplace every morning. When they noticed they were feeling negative they tried to take more responsibility for their emotions by not dumping them on their colleagues. They learned to become much more sensitive to one another's emotional needs.

I asked them what they did when they saw a miserable face posted. Initially they admitted to avoiding the person in question. The VUCA world is tough enough already without having to deal with other people's problems as well, was their reasoning. Funny how we tend to flee from negative emotions in others even though we have all experienced them ourselves.

Slowly, as time passed however, they learned to respond with empathy to the miserable faces and proactively approached the person, asking them if they needed support. They even prepared themselves for an eventual rejection – 'I just want to be left alone' - and learned not to take it personally. They learned to respond with true empathy. 'I can understand you want to be alone considering the way you're feeling. I just want to let you know that if you need someone to talk to I'm here for you.'

This conscious act of silently declaring feelings created a profound bond between these workers. They became more conscious and caring towards one another over time. They felt they could go to work without a mask because they trusted it was safe to share their real selves.

The Utter Importance of our Feelings and Needs
So many of our problems in organisations result from us not being open with one another and not telling each other the truth. Many cultures teach us that 'being emotional' is inappropriate because it's unprofessional and interferes with our rationality. As a result we slowly become 'feelings illiterate'. And yet it is through our feelings that we most deeply connect with one another.

Emotional Literacy – The Vocabulary of Feelings
How comfortable are you about openly sharing your feelings with colleagues at work? How often to you hear reference to feelings in your workplace?
   'This is really uncomfortable for me to say ...'
   'I'm anxious about the outcome of this meeting'
   'I feel nervous about presenting these facts'
   'I'm really worried about this situation'
   'We're uncomfortable with this decision'
   'I'm frustrated about the outcome of that conversation'
   'I'm disappointed with our performance'
   'I'm delighted with your progress'
   'We're thrilled with the news'

Naming and sharing feelings

Time and again I have noticed how 'feelings illiterate' we are. When running the Cultural Diversity edition of The 5 Chairs programme I simulate culture shock in the training room. The participants meet a group of people who are culturally very different to themselves with very different customs and behaviours. The first meeting is embarrassing and destabilising and the participants experience the feelings which normally accompany culture shock. In the debriefing session, when I ask them how they *felt* during the meeting, they usually come up with comments such as, 'They were rude', 'They were cold', 'We tried to talk to them but they didn't answer', 'I wouldn't want to work with them'. None of these are feelings. They are intellectual diagnoses of the behaviours they experienced. When I invite the participants to be more precise and describe only their feelings, the repertoire offered is usually limited to just five or six adjectives such as 'embarrassed', 'uncomfortable', 'surprised', 'annoyed' or 'frustrated'. We are educated to be in our heads and out of touch with our hearts.

The conscious act of recognising and naming our negative emotions substantially reduces their hold over us. If they go unrecognised, we're in their grip and they will take us over. Informing others of the way we feel brings clarity to situations and reduces any ambiguity that usually leads to misunderstandings and conflict. You can argue with someone's thoughts but you can't argue with their emotions.

So why don't we share them more often, and what price do we pay by not sharing them? Unexpressed feelings tend to fester inside us and turn into punishing behaviours or acts of vengeance. These behaviours ultimately destroy relationships.

What happens when we openly express our positive emotions? Their beneficial nature multiples and has a contagious effect on everyone around.

Beware: Responsible Expression of Feelings

There is a deep responsibility attached to the expression of our feelings. We must be careful not to dump them on to others with accusatory language such as 'You made me angry', 'They made me confused', 'I feel misunderstood', 'I feel ignored', or 'It's your fault if I'm not happy.'

Real ownership of our feelings looks more like this:

> 'I got confused when they spoke so fast' (instead of 'They made me confused').
> 'I got angry when you talked to the boss about …' (instead of 'You made me angry').
> 'I feel frustrated when no one asks for my opinion' (instead of 'I feel ignored').

A word of warning here. We always need to check that our intentions are sincere when sharing our feelings with others. If there is any note of manipulation involved, people usually pick it up and trust will be broken.

Practice – Name the Feeling

Practise sharing your feelings more with people around you. Begin at home. When you feel the emotions rising declare them transparently rather than hiding them. Don't expect your family to read your mind. Let them know how you're feeling in a sincere way. Always check there is no hint of punishment or complaint in your voice as you do so. Take full responsibility for the feelings you are experiencing rather than blaming others. Observe the results. See if people open up more to you. Then try it at work.

The Language of Needs

Once we are conscious of our feelings, the next step is to become conscious of our needs. It is not common practice for us to talk about our needs. We usually receive a lot of cultural training that makes us believe it's shameful to have needs let alone declare them. On the contrary, making sacrifices is expected of us. And anyway, we wouldn't want to be thought of as needy, would we? Needy people are judged negatively.

Marshall Rosenberg's powerful Non-Violent Communication process turns this belief on its head. It shows us how feelings and needs are deeply interconnected. The central teaching of NVC is *that feelings are the manifestations of what is happening to our needs*. In other words, when our needs are being met, we experience pleasant feelings and when are needs are not being met, we experience unpleasant feelings.

It therefore follows that the more we are aware of our unmet needs, the easier it is to look for a strategy to get those needs met, either by ourselves or by requesting the collaboration of others.

Important Note. We are more likely to get our needs met if we refrain from telling people *what is wrong with the*m and choose instead to talk about what *we need to feel better*.

The Vocabulary of Needs and Needs Consciousness

Look at the list of needs below and imagine how you would feel if many of them were not met in your life. These unmet needs are the cause of all our negativity.

Autonomy
freedom
choice
independence
self-empowerment
individuality
solitude

Nurture
warmth
caring
tenderness
touch
physical affection
comfort
bonding
emotional safety
relaxation

Integrity
self-worth
self-respect
authenticity
honesty
purpose
vision
dreams
values

Interdependence
respect
fairness
consideration
connection
cooperation
empathy
trust
reassurance
certainty
equality
tolerance
justice
appreciation
being heard
honour
love
acceptance
being liked
predictability
consistency
reliability
contribution
serving
friendship
sharing
intimacy
recognition
validation
community
home and family

Mental
stimulation
comprehension
awareness
reflection
analysis
discrimination
clarity
information
consciousness

Self-Expression
creativity
growth
mastery
goals
meaning
healing

Celebration of Life
play
humour
passion
excitement
pleasure
delight
movement
exercise
stimulation
intensity

Spiritual Energy
harmony
peace
beauty
aesthetic
inspiration
order

Physical Survival
rest
shelter
safety
protection
air
water
food
sex

The more we think about our needs and the more we talk about them, the more aware we are of their importance in our lives. By that I mean, if our happiness depends on getting our most important needs met on a regular basis we need to focus more energy on finding out
- a) what these needs are, and
- b) proactively discovering how to get them met, rather than just complaining.

What are your most important needs?

Your Needs List

A useful exercise for us all to do is write a list of what we think is really important to us in our lives and what we are not prepared to compromise on. Look at the list and choose your top ten most important needs, the needs which drive your life and which you will not compromise on. If you are unconscious of these you might find yourself in situations where you say 'yes' to requests where really you want to say 'no'. Then you'll be in trouble. You create internal confusion and ambiguity and probably start punishing the very person you said yes to.

Many times in companies when I work with dysfunctional teams or with competing functions, one of our very early activities is a transparent and structured exchange around the needs of each team member or each function. Talking about our needs is non-threatening. Talking about what is wrong with others, on the other hand, creates unproductive defensive mechanisms.

Helping individuals and groups consciously identify their individual and collective needs provides the basis for healthy negotiation.

Linking Feelings and Needs

The next step in the process is to link our feelings to our needs. Below are some typical feelings we experience when our needs are a) being met and b) not being met.

a) When our needs are being met:

Happy	Excited	Peaceful	Loving
satisfied	inspired	calm	warm
joyful	energetic	content	appreciative
proud	interested	relaxed	affectionate
confident	involved	serene	sensitive
relieved	amazed	secure	compassionate
touched	amused	clear	grateful
optimistic,	eager	relieved	trusting
stimulated	alert	satisfied	
curious	enthusiastic		

b) When our needs are not being met:

Sad	Scared	Mad	Confused
distressed	afraid	angry	perplexed
despondent	anxious	hostile	frustrated
discouraged	nervous	agitated	embarrassed
disappointed	suspicious	annoyed	reluctant
lonely	sceptical	resentful	hesitant
apathetic	apprehensive	upset	worried
helpless	jealous	bitter	distant
	envious	displeased	
		pessimistic	

Tired	Uncomfortable
exhausted	uneasy
indifferent	ashamed
bored	guilty
lazy	impatient
lethargic	irritated
overwhelmed	hurt
numb	miserable
sleepy	

Needs consciousness in action

What does the combination of expressing feelings and needs look like in practice? The base model of Rosenberg's Non-Violent Communication approach provides us with a powerful structure to follow.

There are four factors we need to take into consideration when linking our feelings to our needs:

1. our observation of the event
2. our feelings
3. our needs
4. a request or strategy to meet our needs

Observation: What did the person/people do? What was the situation? (This must be purely descriptive, not judgmental)
Feelings: How did I feel?
Needs: What is important for me? What needs are met or not met?
Request or Strategy: How can I get those (unmet) needs met in the future?

Let's look at two examples.

1) When my needs ARE being met

Observation: My boss thanked me for my contribution to the project
Feelings: I feel happy, grateful and valued
Needs: My need for recognition and appreciation has been met
Request or Strategy: I'll continue to work with the same level of commitment

2) When my needs are NOT being met

Observation: My boss doesn't give me feedback about my work so I don't know how well I'm doing
Feelings: I feel frustrated, disappointed and sad about that
Needs: It's really important for me to become more proficient at my job. Right now my need for growth and personal development is not being met
Request or strategy: I need to talk to my boss (instead of complaining about her at the coffee machine!). I'll make an appointment with her to have a specific conversation about my performance. I'll explain how important it is for me to develop my skills and ask if she's willing to give me some specific feedback about my performance every two months.

To your boss:
'Thank you for seeing me. I wanted to talk to you about my work. I've been here for nine months now and it's really important for me to know if my work is up to standard and where I need to improve. I'd really value your opinion. Would you be willing to give me some feedback?'

Here we focus on *what we need rather* than what our boss is *not doing*. We concentrate on expressing *what is important for us*. We also have a practical request in mind to help our boss successfully meet our needs. **This change of focus completely revolutionises the way we communicate with one another**.

When we want to get our needs met, the most effective way is by starting with:

> It's really important for me ... / that I ...
> It's really important for me to grow professionally. Would you be willing ...
> It's really important I understand the process. Could you ...

Don't be tempted to get your needs met with ...**You don't / You didn't** ...This will make the other person defensive and the purpose of the conversation is lost.

We have no control over our boss's response to our request for feedback but by openly declaring our needs in a way that our boss hears no judgment of their own behaviour, we increase the likelihood of their collaboration.

This way of combining the language of feelings and needs exponentially increases our likelihood of understanding and collaboration.

The Power of Vulnerability
Another quality desired in The Detect Chair is the courage to show our vulnerability. Put up your hand if you think vulnerability is a form of weakness.

This is a question I always ask my participants on The 5 Chairs programme. Many believe it is a form of weakness and comment that: 'vulnerability reveals our inabilities,' 'it shows our inadequacies and our failings,' 'it exposes us to manipulation.' 'It's risky. People can't be trusted. They'll take advantage of you.' 'You need to protect yourself.' Vulnerability gets bad press in the corporate world where being authentic and speaking our truth is usually equated with being naive. There's a common belief that people will take advantage of us and put us at risk if we do so. It's more sensible to activate our defence systems and be guarded and cautious with others. After all, our job is to be experts and provide solutions to problems, not to show our weaknesses.

Why is this? Have you ever tried being open and authentic and then been burned? Once burned, twice shy. If we form a belief early on that vulnerability is painful, that belief can stay lodged in us for the rest of our lives unless we take the courage to revisit it. But to do that requires safe conditions and deep trust, otherwise the risk of further pain is too great.

The author and researcher *Brené Brown* has turned the notion of vulnerability as weakness on its head. After interviewing thousands of people she has discovered that vulnerability is, in fact, one of our most *accurate measures of personal courage* and that manifesting it actually enhances our ability to forge relationships and lead people more effectively. If we consider the behaviours associated with being vulnerable, this makes total sense.

Below are some vulnerable behaviours identified by participants in The 5 Chairs programme and backed up by Brown's research.

Vulnerability is:
- being open and honest, without editing messages
- saying what you mean
- saying 'I'm sorry' for an inappropriate behaviour
- saying 'I don't know' and being ok with it
- saying 'I was wrong'
- sharing delicate personal issues and feeling safe
- letting other people see me as I really am
- not having to change myself just to 'fit in' or 'please'
- initiating a difficult conversation
- listening to feedback with an open heart
- taking risks
- speaking up
- allowing myself to be imperfect
- being truly accountable
- accepting difficulties
- sharing power and responsibility
- dropping the mask

Many of the above behaviours move people's hearts rather than their heads. We are human. We are not perfect. We do not have all the answers. We all make mistakes. Yet in our world we have made it scary to share our inadequacies and personal challenges. We've learned to mask up and leave half of ourselves in the car park before entering our workplaces. Our over-developed sense of competitiveness keeps us from feeling safe enough to express our vulnerabilities.

And yet opening up and sharing our vulnerability sends out a powerful message. It shows that I am bigger than my fear of judgment. It says I'm not afraid to share my more personal self, I want to connect with you at a deeper level. I want to trust and include you. These messages create strong bonds between people.

As humans we know, deep down, that we are wired to connect but we spend life unlearning this chemistry. And yet we also know that when we address our struggles openly and honestly, from a place of strength, this authenticity resonates with us. And when we access this humanity in us, we begin to connect with one another at a much more personal and profound level. We give more freely and we create more abundance.

Have you ever worked for a leader who has had the courage to show their vulnerability? A leader who sought your advice and shared their concerns with you? Someone who wasn't afraid to admit their mistakes and was tolerant of yours? Someone who shared their power generously with you and made you feel valuable and worthy? Someone who was truly concerned about your well-being and professional growth? Someone who risked their job to protect their team?

How did that feel? How common is it in organisations?

It takes a leader with inner strength, courage, stability and awareness to be vulnerable. A person with a strong inner purpose who will not be intimidated or derailed by a small group of opportunists who are intent on sabotaging the very trust that vulnerability can generate.

The impact of low vulnerability
What does a lack of vulnerability look like in our organisations? More often than not, it generates protective and defensive behaviours where communication is either guarded or is over-compensated with extreme politeness. Uncertainty is usually avoided in our workplaces in order to reduce the risk of making mistakes. After all, we wouldn't want to be accused of failure, would we? When prejudice, judgment and criticism begin to permeate our daily conversations, creativity and innovation, which are high-risk activities, are avoided.

For people to enjoy the benefits of vulnerability and feel safe emulating it, organisations need to create safe environments where leaders with courage can model it. Only then will the workforce dare to step into its full potential.

'New Thinking' Practice – Daring
Practise being vulnerable. Contemplate these questions a) on your own b) in your teams:
1) What am I NOT saying that I want to say? To whom?
2) What is stopping me from saying it?
3) What will the consequences be of not saying it?
4) What have I said that I didn't mean to say? What were the consequences?
5) What do I need to do now to remedy the situation?
6) What conversations are we not having as a team that we need to have?
7) Why are we not having them?
8) What do I feel unsafe talking about at work?

Team Vulnerability Exercise
One effective way I have found to help teams lower their barriers and build greater trust with one another, is by helping them share their individual concerns in a structured way.

I recommend this exercise to help teams clear the air and come out of hiding. The impact is powerful and lasting.

Warm the team members up to the session by first putting the subject of vulnerability on the table. Invite them to share their personal opinions about vulnerability. Is it a weakness or a strength? What are vulnerable behaviours for them? What are the risks and benefits of showing vulnerability? Explore the various facets of vulnerability together.

Then invite them to consciously become vulnerable with one other by doing the following exercise.

a) Sit the team in a circle, like a tribe.
b) Put a container in the middle of the circle.
c) Ask each team member to write on a piece of paper a topic that is affecting the team's performance or their own performance, which they have never expressed openly for fear of judgment, shame or embarrassment.
d) Ask everyone to fold their paper and put it in the container. No names are used here.
e) Ask one team member to randomly withdraw one of the papers and read it to the group.
f) Invite the team to consciously note any judgment or comment that arises in themselves as the topic is read out. (Get the team to apply some Thought Choreography from The Wait Chair.) Remind the team that the objective of the exercise is to explore the issue proposed in a vulnerable and open-hearted way. Suspending judgment is essential here. Monitor this with a gentle reminder: 'No Jackals, please!'
g) Ask each team member to explore the selected topic with an open heart. The exercise is about creating a safe place together where each member can open up and connect at a more vulnerable level. Remind everyone about the importance of i) respecting each topic brought to the table, and ii) keeping any Jackal thoughts or behaviours at bay.
h) Continue with the topics until finished. If necessary, plan another session to address all the team's issues. Do not leave any unaddressed. This is time well spent.

This exercise is very powerful for teams. It allows members to voice their deeper concerns in a structured and protected way without any fear or shame of doing so. The role of the facilitator is key to keeping the environment safe and clean for this to happen. Each team finds its own level of comfort initially and this increases with practice. The more deeply people begin to share of themselves, the greater the trust becomes with one another and the stronger the collaboration inside the team. To compete externally you first need to trust internally. This means daring to be vulnerable with one another.

d) The Art of Speaking Up
Coupled with the skill of talking about our needs is the courage to speak up. How

many times have you been at a meeting where you disagreed with what was being discussed and didn't speak up? How many times have you agreed to a deadline that wasn't realistic? Or had a sense that someone was withholding information from you? Or that an unfair judgment was being made of a colleague's work? What is the cost to you, the team and the company for not speaking up?

It's not always easy to be authentic. It involves taking a risk. How will I be perceived? What will others think? Is it safe to say this? Will it be used against me? It can be especially hard if there are power differentials at play. However, once information is out on the table, it's much easier to find effective solutions, create buy-in, and identify clear, doable steps to achieve objectives.

Finding our voice and speaking up in life is intrinsically linked to our sense of confidence and our feelings of self-worth. In The Self-Doubt Chair we explored the negative impact that self-doubt and toxic silence can have on ourselves and our organisations. In The Detect Chair we develop the antidote to this mindset. We learn to overcome our fear, break our silence, acknowledge our power and take the first step to speak our truth with conviction, diplomacy and respect.

In The Detect Chair we begin to develop our assertiveness. We learn to stand up for our own rights and speak our mind whilst also respecting the needs of others. This requires an ability to:

a)   express our ideas and feelings in an open, direct and honest manner.
b)   stay calm, be curious, ask questions and separate facts from opinions
c)   take responsibility for ourselves and our reactions without blaming or judging others
d)   create healthy boundaries and make sure they are respected
e)   commit to finding a solution when conflict arises

Finding the Courage to Go First

Many misunderstandings at home and in organisations result from our dysfunctional communication. We're all guilty of this. When we avoid facing our differences openly, they get brushed under the carpet ready to explode again at any time in the future.

It really does take courage to proactively address our raw feelings and our unspoken issues but it is the only way to keep our organisations and families emotionally 'clean' and healthy.

When I hear phrases like 'We're not speaking anymore,' 'I haven't spoken to my father for two years,' 'I refuse to work with her,' 'That's the last time I do anything for them,' my heart sinks. Life is full of opportunities for us to share our pain and resolve our differences. It takes practice and skill. Often we just don't know where to start. We're at a loss for words. When we're consumed by emotions we prefer to give up, blow up or shut down.

Dealing with Rising Emotions

Finding ways to deal with our emotions as they are rising is a vital step to staying connected with one another in conversation. At the first signs of the emotions rising in us, we need to acknowledge them and name them. As we said before, naming the emotion automatically reduces its power over us.

I have found the following phrases and questions very effective to help us stay compassionate when we are being triggered by one another. They help us get out of the emotion so that we can take some distance, refocus and return to more rational thinking and behaviour.

a) Recognising the other person's emotion:
I can see this is upsetting you.
You seem concerned about ...
You seem sceptical.
You look a bit perplexed.
Are you worried?
Are you disappointed?

b) Recognising your own emotional impact on others:
I think I've upset you, which wasn't my intention ...
I must have said something out of place. Sorry.
Have I hurt your feelings?
Have I offended you in some way?
Did I misunderstand?

c) Recognising shared emotions:
I can see we're both exhausted. Let's come back to this another time.
Are we both over-reacting to the situation?
We probably need to take a break and get some distance.
What do you think?
The conversation's getting a bit heated. How about taking a break to clear our minds?
Are we losing our way here?

The more we manage to verbalise our emotions by openly describing them in real time, the less they will come between us.

WARNING: *This will only work if your true intention is to connect with the other person. Any sign of manipulation or of using a communication 'technique' will seriously sabotage the trust with the other person.*

Managing our Boundaries and Learning to say 'No'.

'To thine own self be true'
Shakespeare

I first encountered the concept of managing our boundaries on a course in England where I was training to be a Global Executive Coach. I hadn't consciously explored personal boundaries until then. At that time I tended to be a people-pleaser, constantly trying to accommodate other people's needs, often at my own expense. Not wanting ever to appear selfish, I would relegate my own personal needs to the back burner, time after time, and ended up with the crumbs. Saying 'no' to requests wasn't part of my daily vocabulary. And anyway, how would I amass my performance points if I said no to others? People were happy to exploit my boundaries. They didn't know I had any. I allowed my boundaries to be violated because I never declared them! That all changed with one episode.

Early on in my career, I decided to take a break from my overly busy training schedule and spend a two-month period in Sicily working as a G.O. (Gentile Organizzatrice) with Club Med. It was a great opportunity to brush up both my language and entertaining skills. My job wasn't overly taxing. I had to sell beads (the Club Med currency), look after the guests and be part of the entertainment team. My boss was a youngish French man. He was a veteran G.O. and Club Med was his whole world. He was gay and very entertaining. I liked him a lot. We got on well. Or so I thought.

It was the beginning of the season and the Club was doing auditions to allocate special roles to people for the season. As an experienced semi-professional jazz singer and drama graduate, I was chosen to do the poolside cocktail hour and was given some leading roles in the night time shows. I was delighted. Music and theatre are passions of mine. Three weeks into my contract I was doing well. I was attentive and popular with guests to a point where people were coming to me as their point of reference rather than my boss. No request was too much trouble for me. I was doing a good job. So I thought!

Then the problems started. I was victim to a series of acts of sabotage which culminated in losing my role as poolside singer to my boss. (I hadn't known at the time that he was also a singer.) My performances in the evening were also reduced and to top it all, one morning when I turned up for duty at the poolside, I opened my locker to discover that all my beads, worth €800, had disappeared. You can imagine what I felt on discovering this.

I turned to the bar where I knew I would find solace from the kind barman I had made friends with, only to find my boss and his right hand woman leaning on the counter watching me with an expression across their smiling faces which read, 'And now what?' They were visibly revelling in my shock. The experience knocked me sideways. It was daylight conspiracy. Much later I understood that my success as a G.O. in the club was a direct threat to my boss's ego and this was meant as a strong warning to me. I was dumbfounded, devastated and incredulous. My boundaries had been seriously violated. I was at a loss as to what to do.

Should I roll up like a hedgehog and lie low? Should I Jackal away to myself and others about him behind the scenes? Should I confront him directly? This was my call. Life was offering me the chance to step up. My sense of worth and integrity was on the line.

What now seems the obvious thing to do – to have a crucial conversation with him – was nowhere on my radar then. I was rotating through fight, flight and freeze. So many confused and contradictory thoughts.

Defining moments

With hindsight I realise it was a defining moment for me. Life often presents us with these. They are tests which reappear until we are ready to face them. I had a choice. I could call on my inner strength, set my boundaries and let them be known or give my power away, recoil and lay myself open to more violation.

My mind went on a rampage for forty-eight hours, in and out of Jackal and Hedgehog. I hadn't yet created The 5 Chairs so I wasn't aware of my own mind dynamics. I was just caught up in them! I felt angry, dejected, isolated, indignant, impotent, disillusioned. How dare he? How dare they? This is outrageous. Why me? Why are they picking on me? What's wrong with me? How could I have failed? I thought we were friends. Did I really lose all the beads?

I was consumed by confusion, desperately seeking clarity and relief. I knew I had to defend my integrity but I was full of fear. I didn't know where to start. The lesson I needed to learn was boundary setting. I needed a crucial conversation with my boss but I didn't have any notion of how to conduct it.

Luck had it that I had made friends with an Italian bank manager on holiday at the club. He was a wonderfully approachable man and had years of leadership experience behind him, so I decided to confide in him. He masterfully coached me through the predicament and created a safe place in his presence where I could access my fears in a non-threatening way. The conversations I had with him had a profound impact on me. They were my first lessons in assertiveness. Still today in my workshops I refer to him affectionately as being an example of the tangible transformative power that supportive leadership can have.

Talking with him made me realise I had the right to set personal boundaries. We talked about what was acceptable for me and what was not and how it was my responsibility to communicate that directly and honestly to others. I learned that if we don't establish our own boundaries, our sense of worth will be derived from other people. I began to realise that saying 'no' is more about protecting oneself rather than rejecting someone else and that a certain amount of selfishness is necessary in order to establish healthy boundaries. I later observed that those who have weak boundaries tend to violate the boundaries of others.

I summoned up my courage, approached the Head G.O. and asked if I could talk to him. Following the advice of my Italian friend, I expressed my concern about not finding the beads and that I had always been very careful and couldn't imagine how they could have disappeared like that. I also asked if there was something I was doing which wasn't meeting his expectations. He refrained from answering and just quizzed me about how

I expected to replace the beads.

Despite my disappointment at the outcome of the conversation, I was happy to have confronted the situation head on. I was learning a new life skill. The sabotage continued in subtle ways, like acid rain. It reached a point where I felt obliged to escalate it to the Club Director. I described the bullying I was being subjected to, expressed my discomfort and disappointment, and expressed my intent to leave if it continued. On hearing this, he called a three-way meeting with myself and the Head G.O. This was another crucial conversation. Things were aired but no conclusion was reached. Despite this, the Club Director asked me to stay, which I did, but the trust had gone. The bullying stopped but my heart had hardened.

On my last day at the club, I was not asked to pay for the lost beads. My perpetrators backed down. They behaved as though it had never happened. I felt raw inside. Unpleasant as that whole experience felt, it taught me an invaluable lesson. When people cross the line, you owe it to yourself to speak up.

Preparing to say 'No'
There will always be times in life when we need to say 'No'. So often in the work place we will be asked to do things which are outside our official role description. Managing these requests requires finding the balance between wanting to help others whilst also protecting ourselves against overwhelm. If we decide to say No, the skill is to learn how to say No to the task but Yes to the person. If the other person senses we're saying No to them personally, they are more likely to judge us negatively and become unhelpful.

Here are four questions to ask ourselves before saying 'Yes' to someone's request:
1. *Do I really want to do this?*
2. *What does this person really need?* - Find areas of flexibility.
    Check priorities.
3. *If I say 'no' to this person can their needs be met in other ways?*
    By another person? At another time?
4. *How can I support this person to have their needs met?* Define the larger
    goal and look for common interests and needs.

Building our Conversation Intelligence
A twenty-first century conversation:
    Person A: *How are you today?*
    Person B: *Read my blog*

Our lives are made up of countless conversations. Conversations drive our relationships. Poor conversations lead to ambiguity and inefficiency. Effective conversations increase collaboration, drive efficiency and ultimately generate profit. It is clear, therefore, that our ability to lead conversations successfully is central to the success of any organisation and any home. Companies are basically hundreds of conversations which are translated into processes, procedures, products, services, and profit. Or not, as the case may be.

How often do we take the time to check the 'quality' our conversations? How aware are we of the impact our conversations are having on ourselves and others?

So often conversations in the workplace are about either trading information or trying to win points. Comments are fleetingly exchanged in corridors. Requests are made with demand energy. Despite our best intentions, we tend to listen superficially, jump quickly to conclusions and just wait for the opportunity to butt in and assert our own opinions. Then if things heat up and we feel 'triggered', bullets start flying as we defend our stakes. 'That's ridiculous', 'You're wrong'.

So often we polarise and harden into our positions and the person who can 'draw' the fastest or hold their ground the longest, wins. As William Isaacs says in his book *Dialogue and the Art of Thinking Together*; 'We don't listen, we reload.' In this competitive arena we have no time to stop and observe the dynamics of how our conversations unfold. We do, however, feel the full effect of them both physically and psychologically.

So why is it vital that we spend more time exploring this?

Research shows that the quality of our conversational style has a far reaching effect on the general performance of any organisation. When communication flows, we feel respected, valued and safe. Our desire to engage increases and we contribute to our workplace in more creative ways. Failure to converse well, on the other hand, leads to misunderstandings, increased conflict, reduced well-being and poor organisational performance.

The 5 Chairs programme invites us to closely scrutinise how we are managing our conversations on a daily basis and how we can intervene to ensure that they are having a positive impact on the relationships we are building both in our workplaces and at home.

The conversations we hold
Every day we hold a whole range of conversations from simple information exchanges to difficult messages. The level of challenge in any conversation can vary greatly. Below are some examples of typical conversations that take place in the workplace and at home:

>   casual chit chat, information exchange, clarification, inquiry, simple dialogue,
>   sharing opinions, giving positive and negative feedback, making a choice,
>   taking a decision, resolving a problem, agreeing and disagreeing, admitting to
>   a mistake, making a difficult request, delivering bad news, making up after an
>   argument, arguing over an issue.

The more challenging the conversation the more preparation is required.

Breakthrough Conversations
In this section, we will explore how to hold what I call Breakthrough Conversations. These are crucial conversations we hold with other people where the emotional or

political risks are high for everyone and where the outcomes can radically affect us.

We often shy away from these conversations because the risk of failure is high. If handled badly, we might let our emotions get the better of us, exaggerate our communication style, perform badly and end up in conflict. That's why we avoid holding them. However, these challenging conversations are of vital importance and have a significant impact on our lives, but they need careful preparation and skilful management.

The aim of a breakthrough conversation is:
   a)   to explore the differences which separate us
   b)   to discover new ways of reaching a mutual agreement
   c)   to find a strategy to move forward together.

Conversation Blocks
Our conversations are riddled with many types of dynamics. Some are subtle and unconscious, others are blatant and obvious. Many of these dynamics serve either to cover up our real feelings and thoughts or to force our ideas upon other people. We need to be aware of these dynamics and keep them under control in conversation. Look at the following recognised conversation dynamics and identify which you tend to adopt most.

Recognized Conversation Dynamics
Tick the box:
   ❑   *Are you a Subject-changer?*
   If someone brings up a tricky or delicate issue, do you try to change the subject?
   ❑   *Are you a Sidewinder?*
   Do you use indirect ways of sending messages through jokes, side comments, sarcasm or snide remarks rather than saying what you really feel, think or believe?
   ❑   *Are you a Procrastinator?*
   Do you put off answering emails or returning phone calls when you don't want to face an issue with a person?
   ❑   *Are you an Avoider?*
   Do you proactively avoid communicating with people you are having issues with?
   ❑   *Are you a Hider?*
   Do you tend to hold back your real opinion when talking about awkward or difficult subjects?
   ❑   *Are you a Softener?*
   Do you use compliments (at times insincere) to soften the blow of the difficult messages you have to send?
   ❑   *Are you an Exaggerator?*
   Do you sometimes exaggerate or amplify your argument in order to get your point across more forcefully?
   ❑   *Are you an Interrupter?*
   Do you resort to interrupting people to bring the attention back to yourself?

❑   *Are you an Exclaimer?*
Do you make forceful 'Jackal' comments about other people's contributions
such as 'You must be joking' or 'That's crazy' or 'That's ridiculous'?
❑   *Are you an Attacker?*
Do you attack or insult people personally if you get heated in a conversation?
❑   *Are you an Abdicator?*
Do you give in to other people who are forceful?

All of these dynamics are common in communication. They constantly interfere with
the flow of our conversations and create ambiguity around our intentions. Knowing
which ones we personally use to derail conversations is essential to improving our
communication efficacy. The more conscious we are of the dynamics at play, whether
initiated by ourselves or someone else, the more effective our conversations will
become. We owe this to ourselves.

Holding Breakthrough Conversations
Knowing how to hold Breakthrough Conversations can radically improve many areas
of our lives, at work, at home and in society in general. To become skilful at it we
need three things.
   Consciousness - about what our real intentions are when entering a conversation
   Preparation - to structure our thoughts and language when delivering our ideas
   Presence - to manage our emotional reactions during the conversation

What are the 4 characteristics of Breakthrough Conversations?
1. They are RISKY
   Here are some examples of potential breakthrough conversations:
   - drawing attention to a colleague's poor work performance
   - addressing a team member who isn't keeping their promises
     and commitments
   - giving feedback to a boss about their behaviour
   - talking to a team member about their annoying behaviour
   - delivering bad news to someone
   - standing your ground in a decision-making process
   - establishing boundaries with someone who makes suggestive
     or offensive comments
   - saying 'No' to someone or some situation
2. DIFFERENCES OF OPINION are significant
   - the level of misalignment or disagreement between the players is high.
3. They are EMOTIONAL
   - the players have a high emotional attachment to the outcome
     and can quickly move into strong emotional states typical of The Attack
     and The Self-Doubt Chair.
4. They are IMPORTANT.
   - the players have a high personal investment in the content of the
     conversation.

What we need to do is develop an **Early Warning System** to help us recognise when a conversation is becoming difficult. How do you usually react when your emotions begin to build?

Does your heartbeat increase, does the temperature of your skin increase, do you slowly turn red in the face, do your ears turn red, does you stomach churn, do your hands perspire? What happens to your voice? How does your behaviour change in general? Do you engage in any Jackal mind games or do you withdraw and go silent?

These are the signs we need to look out for. Once we are aware of our own reactions we can better manage them. We will also be able to recognise them more easily in our counterpart which will help us reduce the tension.

How can we prepare for a Breakthrough Conversation?
Preparation is crucial. Many of my coaching sessions with executives revolve around how to conduct key conversations with fellow workers across all levels of the hierarchy. To hold successful conversations we need to first explore what I call our conversation influencers. These make up the first module of a 3-Phase Conversation Intelligence module I have developed in tandem with The 5 Chairs programme.

Conversation Influencers
Before entering a Breakthrough Conversation with anyone, it's useful to ask ourselves a series of questions which explore factors that could potentially influence and condition the way we conduct ourselves during the conversation.

These questions address *five specific areas* which, when addressed, give us greater clarity about our intentions.

Step One: PRE-CONVERSATION QUESTIONS
Bias and History
- Am I holding any bias towards this person?
- What stories am I telling myself about this person? How true are they?
- What history do I have with this person?
- What is the present state of our relationship?
- What approach will be most effective with this person?
  (direct, indirect, emotional, rational, analytical, etc.)

Assumptions
- Is this person facing any particular challenges in their life at the moment?
- What are their expectations, abilities, needs, blind spots?
- Am I making any false assumptions about their level of knowledge
  and expertise related to the topic to be addressed?
- How am I expecting the conversation will go?

Intentions
- What is my real intention here?
- What impact do I want to have?
- What is my desired outcome - the benefit to me?
- What is the desired outcome of the other person, the benefit to them?
- What is the desired outcome for the relationship?
- How much of myself do I want to reveal or invest?
- What is the most important message I need to deliver?

Emotional / VUCA factor
- How am I feeling about the conversation? Confident? Anxious? Threatened?
- What is my general state? Am I steady? Under pressure? Nervous? Emotional?
- What emotional reactions can I expect to have during the conversation?
- What emotional reactions can I expect the other person / people to have?

Preparation
- What is the right timing for this conversation? (if not in real time)
- What style of language do I need to use? (assertive, persuasive, factual, emotional?)
- Do I need to adapt my language to this person in order to ensure mutual understanding? (level of expertise, non-native language speaker?)
- Where might I risk using judgmental rather than descriptive language?
- Do I need to adapt my behaviour to create a safe environment for the conversation?
- Who else needs to know I'm having this conversation?
- Do I need any support in this conversation?

Step Two: THE CONVERSATION – The 5 Chairs

As we move into the conversation itself, we need to manage our emotions as best as possible in real time. If the conversation is crucial and the stakes are high, emotions can easily take over. This is where The 5 Chairs come into play. We need to be mindful of any negative thoughts and behaviours that may emerge from the Attack or Self-Doubt Chairs. These could potentially sabotage our intentions. We need to focus on activating all the skills of the Wait, Detect and Connect Chairs to ensure a successful outcome.

Step Three: POST-CONVERSATION QUESTIONS

At the end of any breakthrough conversation it's important to conduct a sort of post-mortem to help us check how effective it was in order to identify any residual issues to be addressed and to gather any lessons learned.

Success Factor for Me?
Was this conversation successful for me?
Did I achieve my intention?
Did I manage my emotions and judgments appropriately?
What didn't I say that I wanted / needed to?
What did I say that I didn't want to?

Success Factor for Them?
Was the conversation successful for the other person / people?
Have their needs been met?
Did they leave with any unanswered questions?
Are they emotionally 'clean' after the conversation (i.e. not bearing any grudges?)

Toxic Residue
Has the conversation left any 'toxic' residue in me? Any residual emotions?
Any doubt, bitterness, sadness, anger, irritation?
What do I need to do to clean my system?

Learnings
What have I learned from this conversation?
In hindsight, is there anything I would have done differently?

Action plan
What action do I need to take now?
Do I need to revisit the conversation or do any remedial work?
Can I confidently move forward?

My clients have found this approach very effective. Exploring important conversations in detail before holding them creates intention, bring clarity and builds confidence. Having heightened awareness exponentially increases our probability of staying rational when strong emotions arise.

I dedicate a significant amount of time to the skill of holding breakthrough conversations on The 5 Chairs programme. It is a fundamental skill for effective living.

A Word of Warning about The Detect Chair
As we develop our ability to speak up in The Detect Chair, our confidence and assertiveness will increase. As this happens, we need to become extremely vigilant. The boundary between being assertive and becoming aggressive or obnoxious is thin. If we are not attentive, we can find ourselves slipping back into The Attack or Self-Doubt Chairs. Assertiveness is about being determined and firm as well as respectful and diplomatic. There is no element of aggressiveness in true assertiveness.

Concluding Thoughts – The Detect Chair
The self-awareness we develop in The Detect Chair feeds our confidence and efficacy in life. We are all leaders. We are constantly leading other people, whether children, colleagues, friends, spouses, parents. This is a sobering thought. I offer you the following guardian angel questions to regularly ask yourself at work and at home. They are designed to keep us aware of what we're wanting to achieve in every moment.

1. What is my **intention** here?
2. What **impact** am I having?
3. What is **right** about this person / this situation?
4. Am I **inspiring** or **engaging** this person right now?
5. Am I **dumping** or **delegating**?
6. What do they say about me **when I'm not here**?

The Detect Chair is not about taking control over others or pushing with our egos. It's not about dumping emotions or subtly punishing others. It's about positively asserting our needs and speaking our truth firmly, in a self-referential way and with respect for others. The Detect Chair is the cornerstone of conscious leadership.

CHAPTER SEVEN
CHAIR 5 – THE CONNECT CHAIR – The Giraffe

The last of the five chairs is The Connect Chair. It's indigo, a colour which represents wisdom, clarity and insight. This is a noble chair from which we manifest truly inclusive behaviours towards one another. It is a chair we all need to aspire to at work, at home and in life in general. It brings balance, harmony and understanding into the world.

The emotional literacy we develop in The Detect Chair lays the foundation for The Connect Chair. The driving force here is empathy, the heart of all collaboration and civility. This chair offers the key to solving conflict whether in the boardroom, in the family or in society at large. It is the best peace pill we have.

In The Connect Chair our focus moves away from ourselves and on to other people. The overarching questions we ask in this chair are:

'What is important for the other person?' 'What do they need?'

Our nudge metaphor in this chair is the Giraffe. This magnificent gentle giant is highly sociable and peaceful. In fact, it is so social it has no territories. It has the biggest heart of all land animals and its long elegant neck enables it to have an unsurpassed vision of the jungle. Its instinctive behaviour is to connect and protect and it's appreciated for its intuition and flexibility. What better metaphor for The Connect Chair?

A touch of empathy
As we move into The Connect Chair we transition into the world of empathy.

> *'Nobody cares how much you know until they know how much you care'*
> Theodore Roosevelt

Imagine yourself in the following situation. You've had a tough week. Things haven't gone well with a client. You've been on a long-haul flight and you're suffering from jet lag. It's 12 noon. You turn up at your hotel looking forward to some comfort and respite, at last! You go to check in and you're informed that your room is not ready. This is the last straw! It's midday, for God's sake! What's wrong with this place! Your Jackals are up. You are visibly frail and fraught, not on your best behaviour and some demand energy in your voice is pushing for preferential treatment from the receptionist.

Imagine receiving the following two different reactions from the receptionist:

a) I'm sorry, Madam, but we can't check you in until 14.30. If you'd like to take a seat while you wait.

or

b) I'm so sorry for the inconvenience, Madam. I can imagine you've been travelling long distance and feel exhausted. You must be wanting to freshen up. We're just waiting for the other guest to check out. It shouldn't take long. I'll make it my priority to take care of the matter. In the meantime would you like to relax in the lounge and we'll serve you a drink and some refreshments of your liking while you wait.

How would you feel after each message?
What makes the difference here?
How long does it take to say b)?

It takes only about 15 seconds to give the second answer but the impact is decidedly more connecting. It shows caring. We feel seen, understood and nurtured. It influences our emotional state and there's a good chance that we will calm down and collaborate more. This type of empathy is healing.

But wouldn't any well-trained professional do this, I hear you ask? What's so unusual? In my experience of working with the service industries, in particular with hospitality and retail, this is not at all common practice. What is unusual about this example are the phrases: 'I imagine you've been travelling and feel exhausted. You must be wanting to freshen up.' So often this is missing from the client experience. What I regularly observe when working in retail and hospitality, is a tendency for staff to move very quickly and automatically into solution mode with their clients, completely bypassing the opportunity for empathising. Why? In the workplace we are trained to 'fix' problems quickly. But how often do we sacrifice that unique chance to really connect with the client and make them feel truly 'seen' and 'understood' before fixing their problems?

Empathy is that touch of magic which creates relationship alchemy. It can really make a difference.

The magic of empathy
I recently returned home to Cambridge to visit my parents. My father was recovering from a hip operation and one evening we decided to dine out. It was a Friday night and he was beginning to feel confident enough to walk out. We booked a table at a restaurant which my parents occasionally frequent. We purposely decided to have an early dinner to avoid the crowds.

On arrival at the restaurant my heart sank. There was a hen party in full swing and the decibels were flying. They were, needless to say, having great fun. However, my father who's in his nineties and hard of hearing experiences great discomfort when the surrounding environmental noise is high. Our table was reserved right behind the ladies! We had a choice: to move tables or change restaurant. The waiter was obliging, so we stayed.

As we moved through the restaurant to another table at the back we were greeted by a new waiter. I was immediately struck by his warm, friendly demeanour and welcoming smile. We were seated and immediately handed the menus, served water and provided with bread. What ensued could have tested any waiter's patience. Or not, depending on their ability to deal with life's imperfections and annoyances.

The restaurant was dimly lit and the overhead lamp at our table was broken. This didn't help matters. I could see my father was struggling to read the menu. Just as

I was noticing, the waiter, who had read the concern on my face, quickly extended his hand, armed with an iPhone on torch mode and held it over my father's menu. A thoughtful gesture which I acknowledged gratefully. I pulled out my own phone to relieve him of his duty but couldn't find the torch mode. I realised I'd never used it before! Feeling a little embarrassed at my ignorance in front of a millennial and on the point of becoming impatient with myself, the young waiter was quickly at my side with a 'Can I help you, madam?' I passed him my phone and instead of just fixing the problem he leaned over and talked me through how to find it.

In the meantime my mother wasn't happy with her seating arrangements. She was frowning and visibly uncomfortable. Part of me was already imagining the messages going to the kitchen. 'Watch out for table 3. Troublemakers!' Noticing again my mother's discomfort and not showing a hint of impatience, our waiter immediately suggested swapping to the next table where things would suit us better. With a smile on his face he transferred everything in seconds. Nothing was too much trouble. I was beginning to wonder what planet he had descended from. Small thoughtful acts, kind attentiveness, no grimaces. He was making the evening a pleasure for myself and my aging parents. He understood both their fragility and my concern.

When we were ready for dessert, I looked around for the young waiter ready for another delightful encounter. He had gone off duty. I immediately felt sad. He had left his mark. With just a few words and gestures and a genuinely caring attitude that young man had moved me.

A little bit of empathy goes a long way in this world. Giving solace solves problems. The Dalai Lama says that just twenty minutes of pure empathy can cure deep-seated pain and suffering.
Years of experience working with many different types of organisations across multiple sectors has taught me that what most eludes us in our workplaces today is empathy. We are living in a hyper-individualist age driven by personal branding and virtual social media communication where our egos are being constantly fed and relationships are valued by the number of followers or 'likes' we are able to amass. This is having an effect on the 'we' factor of our collaboration.

We need to bring back the caring factor into our lives, and especially into our organisations. We're moving so fast that we no longer 'see' one another. Without more authentic connection we seriously risk impoverishing the quality of all our relationships.

Empathy is a challenge for us. It means putting aside our own egos and giving the limelight to others. This is a fairly unintuitive and complicated act for most human beings, especially living in a VUCA world where time is pushing, stress is increasing and individualism is evermore king.

The Connect Chair is all about conscious empathy where we take our relationships to a higher level of understanding and connection. Sometimes all it requires is just a small act of attention and some care coupled with the intention to connect, as shown by our young hero waiter.

So how can we develop this more at work and at home? Some visionary companies are taking the lead. Google, for example, offers mindfulness and empathy training to its employees. In his book Reinventing Organisations, Federic Laloux tracked organisations working with a radically more productive organisational model where people work together in a powerful way by changing their belief systems. Rather than searching for the secret key to gaining market share by beating the competition and increasing profits, these organisations are eliminating power hierarchies and introducing neutral hierarchies and self-organising teams driven by high levels of trust, engagement and self-management. The people in these organisations are truly connected and valued and this is reflected in their exponential success. So much of this success depends on developing an inclusive mindset supported with a strong practice of empathy.

The Dynamics of Empathy

'You never really understand a person until you consider things from his point of view... until you climb into his skin and walk around in it.'
Harper Lee – To Kill a Mocking Bird

Although empathy is slowly coming onto the radar of organisations it is still not extensively practised or considered as a necessary skill to be trained. Why is that?

As mentioned before, empathy tends to clash with individualistic competitiveness and ego-driven desires and behaviours. It is still considered by some as a 'touchy-feely' topic, especially in cut-throat organisations interested primarily in driving results. And yet without it we become emotionally tone-deaf to one another and never fully develop what really drives the success of our organisations: human relationships.
Numerous new studies now directly link the practice of empathy to increased sales and enhanced performance, especially in diverse workforces. So what exactly is empathy?

Empathy and its friends
Whilst researching empathy I was struck by the myriad of differing definitions that exist for it. One thing is quite clear however. Without it, we're in deep trouble. Dr Antonio Damasio has outlined in his book *Descartes' Error: Emotion, Reason, and the Human Brain* that medical patients who have damage to the part of the brain associated with empathy display significant deficits in relationship skills, even though their reasoning and learning abilities remained intact.
For our own purposes with The 5 Chairs, I think it's helpful to make a distinction between sympathy, empathy and compassion with the following definitions.

Sympathy involves expressing feelings of pity, sadness and sorrow for someone else. 'You poor thing! I'm sorry you're going through this'. The focus here is on what's going on in ourselves not in the other person. Sympathy does not demonstrate that we've understood how the other person is feeling and what they are needing. It expresses our own emotional response towards a person, which is not necessarily shared by the person.

Empathy is the ability to understand another person's state of mind by stepping into their shoes and looking at the world through their eyes. It's trying to understand another person's feelings and needs so that we can respond appropriately to what they require, whilst still realising that their pain is not our own.

Compassion is to suffer with someone, to show them concern and feel a strong desire to help alleviate the other person's distress. Compassion is therefore a vital ingredient of empathy.

A Simple Test of Your Daily Empathy
Imagine you're in the station about to catch a train and a homeless person comes up to you and asks you for money. How do you react?

a) Do you get annoyed and move on quickly to catch your train with a 'stop bothering me and why don't you do something useful in your life' attitude on your face?

b) Do you find the situation uncomfortable? Do you become aware of being observed by other people so you get embarrassed, put your head down and speed past avoiding any eye contact?

c) Do you feel bad so you give them 50 cents to alleviate your own discomfort and eliminate any sense of guilt you might have?

d) Do you try to imagine what it must be like living that person's life; being homeless, sleeping out at night and being avoided every day by people who don't understand their predicament? Do you connect to their emotions and feel with them?

e) Do you offer them a coffee or have a conversation with them to understand their situation better and learn about what they most need?

f) Does what you do depend on how you're feeling that day?

If your reaction is d) or e) then you are displaying empathy. You are trying to imagine yourself into the perspective of the other person in order to respond in a way which is appropriate to their needs.

Why is empathy so challenging?
'A human being is a part of a whole, called by us "universe", a part limited in time and space. He experiences himself, his thoughts and feelings as something separated from the rest, a kind of optical delusion of his consciousness. This delusion is a kind of prison for us, restricting us to our personal desires and to affection for a few persons nearest to us. Our task must be to free ourselves from this prison by widening our circle of compassion to embrace all living creatures and the whole of nature in its beauty.'

Albert Einstein

We are all born with the capacity for empathy. Babies display it naturally. And yet by the time most of us are adults we will do anything rather than display our emotional vulnerability or acknowledge feelings which we commonly define as weak.

Mary Gordon, an award-winning educator, child advocate and social entrepreneur has proven this in her groundbreaking educational programme and book, *Roots of Empathy – Changing the World Child by Child*. She is training children across the world, from kindergarten to age fourteen, in the currency of relationship-building by developing their ability to express their emotions, understand another person's and respond empathetically to the expressed emotions of others.

At the heart of Gordon's programme are an infant and parent who visit the classroom every three weeks over a period of a year. A trained instructor coaches the students to observe the baby's development and to label its feelings. In this experiential learning, the baby is the 'teacher' and a lever which the instructor uses to help children identify and reflect on their own feelings as well as the feelings of others. The children are seen as the 'Changers'. As they slowly become more competent in understanding their own feelings and the feelings of others they become less likely to physically, psychologically and emotionally hurt each other through bullying and other cruel activities.

During the programme children actually learn how to challenge cruelty and injustice which arises in their school environment, and research evaluations of the Roots of Empathy programme have indicated significant reductions in aggression in the children and increases in pro-social behaviour. The emotional literacy taught in the programme lays the foundation for safer and more caring classrooms. We have a lot to learn from Gordon's work.

Why then, as adults, has our ability to display empathy been so compromised?
Empathy pushes most of us beyond our comfort zones. When we fully open up to understanding and supporting other people we move into unknown territories where life is no longer 'on our terms'. Unless we are seasoned empathisers, putting other people ahead of ourselves will automatically open us up to uncertainty.

In order to empathise with another person we need to move beyond our biases, prejudices and fixed opinions. Whatever our preferences, we need the confidence to embrace what Pema Chodron calls in her book *Living Beautifully with Uncertainty and Change*, 'the raw, edgy, unpredictable energy of life'. We need to stay curious, show we care and, above all, be innately decent with one another. Empathy also requires we maintain this attitude whether we like the people in question or not. This is a challenge in the workplace where we don't often get the chance to choose our colleagues or fellow team members.

People in the service industries have to call on their empathy every day. Serving others means opening the door to people of all shapes, sizes, colour, behaviours, attitudes, languages, religious and political tendencies, whilst managing yourself in the process. It requires a high level of curiosity for and acceptance of the uneasiness and unfamiliarity that diversity brings with it.

Living Empathy
From my own observations of people who display a high level of empathy, a combination of the following behaviours is at play:

1. **Ego Relegation**
2. **Presence**
3. **Imagination & Perspective Taking**
4. **Empathic Hearing**

1. Ego Relegation
As mentioned before, practising empathy is an act of great generosity. We have to temporarily put our own egos on the back burner and reduce our level of self-importance in order to give what Steven Covey calls 'psychological air' to another person. It requires a 'service' mindset and orientation to practice empathy. In other words, a willingness to be 'of service' to another person as they work though their life discomforts and trigger responses.

How good are we at momentarily letting go of our egos? Can we easily put our own emotions and needs on hold as we explore someone else's?

Our daily conversations tend to resemble taking turns at monologuing rather than really understanding what's going on with the other person. As Covey says, often our priority is 'to be understood by others rather than to understand others'. And even when we intentionally give our attention to another person, how soon is it before our ego thoughts return centre stage and the attention is back on ourselves? Offering empathy to others requires true focus and presence.

2. Presence
> *'Don't just do something. Stand there!'*
> ***Buddha***

When we empathise with someone we need to open up all our communication channels, our ears, eyes, head and heart, in order to deeply understand what they are experiencing and what feelings and needs they are entertaining. The Meerkat's behaviour teaches us that. Watch how attentive and still this small animal can be on sentinel guard.

The Israeli philosopher and psychotherapist Martin Buber said 'presence is the most powerful gift one person can give another'. When we are truly present with another person and completely focussed on what they're feeling or needing, that person can touch deeper levels of consciousness in themselves and reach greater self-understanding. It helps the person release tension, experience relief and often reach resolution. Most of us have experienced this at some time in our lives.

Empathising also requires patience and steadiness. The ability to sit with a person as they cry or as they explode without being embarrassed or self-conscious. The ability to wait for a sign from the other person that their soul-searching is complete and that they are ready to open up again to the world. This can take time, which most of us don't believe we have in this 'I don't have time' mantra world. However as people are our most important asset, this is time well invested. The preoccupations a person can resolve in the presence of another caring presence is ten times more likely than when alone.

Most of us are not naturally skilled at empathising with others. We are more adept at digging for our own needs rather than understanding other people's. However there are practices we can start adopting NOW and which will automatically increase our level of empathy towards others. The first step is to remove our empathy distractors.

Empathy Distractors

When a person is upset, needs to talk or is looking for a moment of respite from their own suffering and confusion, this is a cue for us to move into empathy. Our job is to temporarily accompany that person on a journey into their unknown territories to find some form of relief or resolution. This is no mean feat as we can easily be derailed from our role as empathiser by our own distractions. Here's what we often do when people come to us in trouble.

Advising: 'Why don't you ...' 'I think you should ...'

Explaining: 'As far as I'm concerned that's ...'

Self-referencing: 'That reminds me of a time when I ...'
'Wait until you hear what happened to me!'

Sympathising: 'You poor thing. Well at least you ...'

Minimising: 'Don't worry. You'll soon feel better.'

Correcting: 'I think you misinterpreted that. What they probably meant was ...'

Blocking: 'Come on now. Cheer up. It's not that bad.'

Trumping:'You think that's bad.
That's nothing in comparison with what happened to me!'

Interrogating: 'What happened exactly?' 'How long has this been going on?'

The above reactions arise from a belief that it's our role and responsibility to try and 'fix' someone when they're in trouble. Often we react from the assumption that people don't have the answers to their own problems and therefore need someone else to fix them for them. In reality, what people really need in times of strife is some mental space and a caring presence to access their own solutions.

When we are in a predicament and are trying to understand what's going on inside ourselves, we need to be able to peel away our emotions and thoughts to get to the crux of our dilemma. This is a precious but usually bitty process where we stumble around and meet our uncertainties and our vulnerabilities head on. Sometimes we might need long moments of silence as we are processing our emotions and thoughts. Our concentration can be easily derailed if we perceive that the other person is uncomfortable with our silence and needs to fill it with any of the above distractors to reduce their own embarrassment. When we're working through our 'stuff' we need to know that the person listening to us can sit comfortably with our silence and be patient as we explore. We don't want to worry about tracking their needs when we're in our own process. We need safe, sensitive and steady accompaniment for this.

Can we learn to just stand back and create a safe space for another person as they work through their issues? Can we refrain from jumping in to make them feel better? Can we consciously take care of any discomfort we may be feeling in ourselves in the process? Can we refrain from giving unsolicited suggestions or solutions?

A word of warning.
If you are feeling very distracted, do not offer empathy to another person. It's painful if we perceive the other person is only partially listening to us. We have all experienced the anxiety at sensing that someone doesn't really have the time to hear us.

If someone is in need of your empathy first check how you are feeling yourself before entering into the process. Empathy requires presence, focus, energy and heart. Ask yourself:
Am I feeling calm and receptive?
Am I preoccupied with my own issues?
Can I come fully into the present moment with this person right now?

If you have any doubts, don't even start. You could do more damage than good. Instead, acknowledge the other person's need to talk, show you genuinely want to respond to their need to share and that you understand it's important for them. Explain you want to honour that need but are feeling distracted yourself right now so wouldn't do justice to them. Offer to schedule another time soon to talk when you can give them your full attention. Take full responsibility for your role as empathiser.

Reflecting Back
One practice I learned at a Nonviolent Communication retreat and which I have found to be truly effective in the process of empathising, is that of reflecting back. It is a way of accompanying someone without adding any external thoughts to theirs or

distracting them from their own stream of thought.

A chance to put this into practice presented itself immediately at the end of the retreat on my return to Italy. It was during a phone call with my beloved late 103-year-old godmother. During our conversation she unexpectedly declared, 'I want to die.'

My immediate reaction, prior to doing the NVC course, would have been something along the lines of, 'Don't be silly. Of course you don't! You're just having a bad day, that's all,' or some other pull-yourself-together type comment, mainly uttered to relieve my own discomfort. Instead a little voice inside me stopped me in time saying 'watch the distractors!' I changed track and followed Rosenberg's recommendations.

'So you want to die?' I asked back.

'Yes,' she continued. 'I've had enough of this life. I've had enough of this home. There's no one interesting to talk to here. I get so bored with the same old conversations.'

'So you're missing good conversation, is that it?' I said, staying on her track.

'Yes. And I can't see very well anymore ...my eyesight's getting worse and you know how much I love reading.'

'Yes, you've always been a big reader,' I reflected back.

'Yes. It's my lifeline. I miss reading so much. Especially autobiographies. And now even my hearing's going so I can't listen to the radio either. It's so frustrating!'

'Yes, I can imagine that's frustrating for you,' I repeated.

'Yes it is! I've always listened to Radio 4. You know that. We used to listen together sometimes. It's such a good channel ... (Pause) ... I shouldn't complain though. I'm pretty healthy otherwise.'

'Yes, it's amazing. You've been very healthy all your life really.'

'Yes, that's true now that I think about it ... (Pause) ... Now my dear. How are you?'

After that conversation I recalled how often in the past I had wanted to 'fix' my godmother rather than just 'be' with her. By suspending any sense of personal responsibility to solve her issues, I was able to step into her world and connect to her feelings and predicament more fully. I was able to give her the psychological space she needed to talk 'out' her thoughts and feelings and when she had exhausted them, she naturally returned to more pleasant living by herself. I have often since practised this with people when they need to be heard and found it to be very healing.

I was intrigued to hear from my doctor nephew that this type of empathy practice is now part of patient consultation training in certain medical faculties in England. With the help of professional actors playing the part of patients, trainee doctors learn to dedicate the first part of any consultation to pure empathy, making patients feel safe and cared for before moving onto the diagnosis and cure phases. We could all benefit from a little of this training in our organisations!

A simple practice in Giving Empathy

Next time someone comes to you in difficulty, try the following:

a. Take a big breath, slow down and focus.

b. Consciously recognise the opportunity you have to help another person feel better.

c. Open all channels of listening – ears, eyes, mind, heart.

d. Move into SILENT MODE.

e. BLOCK any empathy distractors.

f. Avoid FIXING the person.

g. Show your attentiveness by occasionally REFLECTING what they are saying.

h. Once the person seems complete, ask if you can help in any other way.

This simple but conscious act can create a deep level of trust between people in a short amount of time. It's also the best way to empower people to find their own solutions.

On the subject of empowerment, I always invite leaders to stop and ask themselves the following questions whenever they are approached by their staff with requests for help.

• What do I want to do here?

• What is my intention? To fix their problem for them or help them find their own solutions and make them more independent and responsible?

Empathy is about understanding other people's needs. Someone who learns to explore their issues and who comes up with two or three possible solutions on their own to discuss with their boss is a very valuable player.

3) Imagination & Perspective Taking Skills

Another essential skill for effective empathising lies in our ability to explore other perspectives. This is the cognitive aspect of empathy. Henry Ford said, "If there is any one secret of success, it lies in the ability to get another person's point of view and see things from their angle as well as your own."

Isn't it true that at times we are so focused on our own objectives that we forget to see the perspective of others?

• Before we click 'send' on an email to our international subsidiary, do we imagine the impact it will have on the receiver?

• As we're about to walk into our next meeting, have we taken a moment to imagine how people are thinking and feeling about the topic of the meeting?

• How often do we truly allow ourselves to be influenced by another person's point of view?

• How often do we really take time to understand the challenges our colleagues are facing in other departments?

Perspective taking is one of the most important, if not the most important, adaptive skills we need to activate when relating to others. When a misunderstanding or conflict arises due to a difference of perspective it is crucial we spend time trying to fully understand each other's viewpoints to reach a constructive outcome. To succeed in doing this, we need to constantly remind ourselves that our aim is to arrive at a destination together. If we dig our heels in and refuse to explore the other person's view or feelings, dialogue quickly degenerates. Perspective taking does not mean agreeing with others, but it does require showing acknowledgment and respect for another perspective. If we can make a practice of doing this, we are more likely to stimulate a similar response in them. To influence others we need first to be open to their influence.

The advantage we have as human beings over the animal world is our extraordinary power of imagination. It's that ability to bring things into mind which aren't present. When we activate our imagination we engage with someone else's consciousness. When we suppress our imagination we also suppress our empathy for others which is how we end up committing terrible acts of violence and war.

There is an indigenous tribe living in the snowy mountains of Victoria in Australia called the Koori Culture. One of their four life tenets is the belief that by expanding our perspective we can eventually reach enlightenment. It is called the *Ya-idt-midtung Philosophy* and it encourages 'a varied perspective' approach to life. They believe:

A varied perspective is the key to perception
Perception is the key to understanding
Understanding is the key to respect
Respect is the key to harmony
Harmony is the key to joy
Joy is the key to enlightenment

The more open we are to other perspectives the more robust our own ideas become. So often, however, when we are under pressure and thinking fast, we don't pay attention to our thinking but revert to default mechanisms, make assumptions and leap to conclusions. These tendencies surely block our access to empathy.

4) Empathetic Listening
Empathy requires extremely vigilant listening skills. It requires we be attentive to all the signs a person is emitting. This is another challenge for our ego. Most of the time, instead of really listening, we are preparing our responses and just waiting for our turn to speak. How often do we consciously monitor our listening skills when we are in conversation?

Empathetic listening involves much more than just registering, reflecting back, or even understanding the words that are said. Communications experts estimate that only ten percent of our communication is represented by the words we say. Another thirty percent is represented by the sounds, and sixty percent by our body language. Empathetic listening requires listening not only with your ears and mind but also with your eyes and heart. As Stephen Covey suggests: 'You listen for feeling and meaning. You listen for behaviour. You use your right brain as well as your left. You sense, you intuit, you feel.'

The Connect Chair invites us to practise this quality of listening with a specific focus. Our attention is not only on the thoughts of the person but more specifically on their feelings and needs. In The Detect Chair we learned to listen to our own feelings and needs. When in trouble, we ask ourselves the question, 'What am I feeling?' 'What is important for me here?' 'What do I need?' We are in a heightened state of self-awareness.

In The Connect Chair we reverse our focus and ask 'How are they feeling? 'What is important for them right now?' 'What do they need right now? Instead of judging or focussing on 'what's wrong' with the other person, we look for a way to empathise with them.

Empathy and Leadership

How important is empathy to be successful as a leader today?

Daniel Goleman in his Harvard Business Review article *'What Makes a Leader?'* identifies three reasons why empathy is so important for leadership:

a)   The increasing use of teams – which he refers to as 'cauldrons of bubbling emotions'
b)   The rapid pace of globalisation and diversity in the workplace
c)   The growing need to retain talent – especially young, independent, highly marketable mobile workers.

'Leaders with empathy' Goleman says, 'do more than sympathise with people around them: they use their knowledge to improve their companies in subtle but important ways,' which doesn't mean agreeing with everyone's views or trying to please people but to 'thoughtfully consider employees' feelings – along with other factors – in the process of making intelligent decisions.'

Research carried out by the Centre of Creative Leadership (CCL) has backed this up, revealing that the nature of leadership is shifting. As diversity increases in our workplaces, leaders now need to create shared alignment and commitment with people not only in the next office or building but also with those from very different histories, perspectives, values and cultures. As a result, much more emphasis is being placed on building and maintaining relationships. Empathy is key to achieving this.

CCL analysed data from 6,731 managers from 38 countries which produced two key findings:

1.   *Empathy is positively related to job performance*

Managers were rated by their subordinates on the following four items using CLL's Benchmarks 360° instrument.

- Is sensitive to signs of overwork in others
- Shows interest in the needs, hopes and dreams of other people
- Is willing to help an employee with personal problems
- Conveys compassion when people disclose a personal loss

The results revealed that empathy is positively related to their job performance and that managers who show more empathy towards direct reports are also viewed as better performers in their job by their bosses. Many of the empowerment skills required of managers, such as coaching, mentoring, giving and receiving feedback, delegating and career planning require a well-developed sense of empathy. It is becoming the foundation of successful leadership in the twentieth century.

2.   *Empathy is especially important in high power distance cultures where a paternalistic leadership approach is preferred (e.g. China, Egypt, Malaysia, Singapore, Taiwan)*

The second finding relates to working across cultures which requires that managers understand people who have very different perspectives and experiences. This can be a real stretch for us. We're often good at accepting differences at a very superficial level, such as enjoying different local cuisines and traditions, but when it comes to sharing best practices and negotiating across different cultures, with different traditions, dimensions, values and behaviours, we need to call on an advanced set of empathy skills.

'Shut up, woman!' – A Call for Empathy

On one of my Cross-Cultural Management editions of The 5 Chairs programme, a young Italian employee shared an experience that had left him speechless. It was during a video-conference session with a counterpart Japanese team.

His Italian team leader presented some financial data to the Japanese team and then handed over to his technical expert, Claudia, to outline some troubleshooting areas which needed addressing in their joint project. After only a few minutes of her analysis, the Japanese team leader intervened with, 'Shut up, woman.' Needless to say, the members of the Italian team were shocked on hearing this. All eyes turned to their leader. Whatever he would choose to do in that moment would radically influence his team, his Japanese counterpart and the business at hand. It was his call.

What would you have done?

There are numerous potential reactions to a situation like this, but one thing is for sure. Getting it right in order to stay at the negotiation table would require a combination of quick thinking, extreme people acumen, cultural intelligence and multi-directional empathy skills.

Let's take this trigger through the five chairs and explore what the reaction could look like from each chair.

Situation: Video conference between an Italian team in Milan and Japanese team in Tokyo

Agenda of meeting: Updating on joint project status

Trigger phrase: 'Shut up, woman' (Japanese team leader to Italian female engineer)

Team leader's options:

Attack		
	Thoughts:	'How dare he talk to Claudia in that way! Who the hell does he think he is. I thought the Japanese were supposed to be kind and polite. That's a joke! This guy needs a lesson!'
	Feelings:	shock, indignation, anger, hostility.
	Reactions:	to challenge, openly criticise the attitude of the Japanese manager, demand an apology, threaten, close the call.
	Impact:	breakdown in communication, strained relations, broken trust, lost collaboration, conflict, no business.

Self-Doubt		
	Thoughts:	'Now what do I do? Help! I wasn't expecting that. I don't know how to handle this. How embarrassing.'
	Feelings:	alarmed, unnerved, embarrassed, exposed, confused, sense of impotence, unsteady.
	Reactions:	to ignore, change subject, avoid conflict, smile nervously.
	Impact:	compromised leadership, Japanese behaviour condoned, team colleague feels betrayed, disrespected and abandoned.

Wait		
	Thoughts:	'Stop. Breathe. Stay calm. Suspend your judgment. Hold the space. What's important here?'
	Feelings:	alert, vigilant, curious, attentive.
	Reactions:	to suspend judgment, choose not to take the behaviour of the Japanese colleague personally, maintain emotional calm and seek rationality.
	Impact:	no negative reaction, no side taking, desire to understand, atmosphere of exchange maintained, avoidance of conflict.

	Detect	
	Thoughts:	'I need to step in here. It's my responsibility to deal with this firmly but diplomatically and move the conversation forward.'
	Feelings:	concern, surprise, responsibility, accountability.
	Needs:	to address the matter consciously, respond appropriately without offending or condoning.
	Reactions:	to display inner purpose, give assertive feedback, understand and explain the different points of view.
	Impact:	to bring clarity and awareness, and reduce tension.

	Connect	
	Thoughts:	'There must be a reason for his behaviour. I need to under stand why he reacted like that. It could be cultural. At the same time I need to support Claudia and build reconciliation between her and our Japanese counterpart in order to move forward.'
	Feelings:	calm, patience, showing empathy and understanding for both Claudia and Japanese colleague.
	Needs:	to maintain connection, to recognise Claudia's role, to recognise differences in cultural gender-related expectations, to see the situation from the Japanese viewpoint
	Reactions:	emotional, social and cultural intelligence
	Impact:	clarity, exposed intentions, reconciliation, continued collaboration.

In response to this trigger the Italian team leader was called on to take a multi-directional empathic approach to maintain all round connection. Quite a task in the split seconds available to him.

He has to a) master his own reaction b) support Claudia and his team and c) give firm but respectful feedback to the Japanese team leader to establish acceptable behavioural boundaries. This requires extreme focus and presence. Reacting from The Attack Chair and The Self-Doubt Chair could have destroyed both the relationships and the business. Another vital ingredient for the successful handling of this particular situation is having some cross-cultural knowledge. An awareness of the gender dynamics in the Japanese culture is essential here. The status of Japanese women is still quite different to that of European women. A more submissive approach is expected of women in the Japanese business context. I asked a Japanese girlfriend and business owner what is expected of Japanese women in a business context and she came up with the following list:

• be modestly dressed – sober and conservative.
• read the silence – have the ability to read the subtlest of signs in communication
• be cooperative – 'discussion' is aggressive, so accept rather than discuss. Don't

disagree openly.
* be indirect – soft approach, soft manners, avoid a direct 'No'.
* women are newcomers – women should not stand out.
* men are the game-setters – follow their lead.
* follow the protocol with respect.

It becomes clear from this list that Claudia's naturally assertive approach could have unintentionally offended the senior Japanese team leader, whose instinctive reaction was to put her in her place. Claudia was also unaware of another important value in the Japanese culture, saving face. Any criticism or negative feedback of the Japanese in public can cause serious loss of face and damage trust. Face is rigorously defended in many Asian cultures and in Japan, where perfectionism is highly valued and failure is generally unacceptable, the treatment of face requires special attention.

What the Italian team leader actually said was, 'If we're going to continue this call I need to ask you to change your tone of voice when speaking to my colleague.' The Japanese leader did adjust his behaviour and the conversation continued, if somewhat icily.

A more complete response from The Connect Chair could be:

'Can we just stop here a moment? [signalling a need to stop and step outside the conversation]. I can see you are irritated with something Claudia said [to Japanese team leader – observing and naming the Japanese team leader's visible emotion]. I can imagine you are not used to dealing directly with a female colleague in these matters [referring to the Japanese cultural protocol]. I'd like you to know that Claudia is our expert in these matters and is a very important member of the team [framing Claudia's value]. I'm certain it wasn't her intention to offend you in any way [defending Claudia's intentions]. She was expressing a concern we have about one of the processes you are using which is incompatible with our system [using objective language and taking joint responsibility for the problem]. Could we look at that now and try to find a way together to ensure maximum efficiency moving forward? [Reinstating collaboration.]

In these moments of complex human interaction where there are multiple perspectives at play, a combination of the Wait, Detect and Connect chair are our best guides. Keeping our heads about us and focussing on the intention to stay connected, despite the emotions at play, requires great skill and considerable practice but usually keeps us moving forward in dialogue.

Concluding Thoughts - The Connect Chair

When The Connect Chair works hand in hand with The Detect Chair the result is a powerful balance of assertive push behaviours and sensitive pull behaviours. The combination of these create behaviours which foster our ability to understand, connect and collaborate with others. Our challenge is to spend as little time as possible in the Attack and Self-Doubt Chairs and concentrate on building the Wait, Detect and Connect skills.

IN CONCLUSION

At the beginning of this book I promised to help you become your own mini-expert in human behaviours and give you some practical ways of modifying the behaviours which are not serving you or your relationships well.

I sincerely hope I have fulfilled that promise for you.

I also invited you to be courageous, patient and disciplined. Courageous enough to step back and question your daily behaviours, patient enough to accept that changing behaviour takes time, and disciplined enough to practise the exercises in this book over and over again until you have achieved your new desired behaviours. Now, at the end of the book, as you step back into your conversations and relationships, I ask that of you again.

It's one thing to read this book; it's quite a different matter to apply its messages. There is no 'quick fix' here. Your commitment is crucial, as is your persistence. As you practise you might come up against years of conditioning. It's normal to meet this with resistance. I guarantee, however, that if you persevere with the exercises and make small changes to your behaviour, you will begin to see a difference in the quality of your relationships and you will notice a radical increase in collaboration around you.

Whenever you're feeling wobbly or about to give up, turn to these questions to nudge yourself back on your way.

> Are my behaviours serving me well?
> Am I in control of my emotions or are they controlling me?
> What would my best self do now?

Take time to play with The 5 Chairs. Use them with your teams, friends and families. Explain them to new people you meet. Refer to them in casual conversation. Use them to give feedback in a playful way. Turn to them for guidance. Embed them into your daily living. Teach them to your kids. (They get it immediately!) Have fun with the animal metaphors. Mention when there's a Jackal in the room. Invite the Hedgehog in yourself and others to uncurl and open up. Emulate the Meerkat when emotions are about to sabotage. Play like the Dolphin. Nurture the Giraffe in you.

My wish for you is that The 5 Chairs will benefit you as much as they have benefitted me. I would like to leave you with a story of how I recently used The 5 Chairs to save me from potentially damaging a precious relationship I was trying to nurture.

> There is a very important young woman in my life called Samira. She is my partner's daughter. Bonding with her was strategic to both my own happiness and my partner's. I decided to organise an evening for just the two of us in Milan, a chance for 'the girls'

to spend a night on the town together. I wanted to surprise her so I booked us into the Blue Note Jazz club in Milan where The Manhattan Transfer were billing. As a baby-boomer I knew I was taking a risk with a 25-year-old millennial but The Manhattan Transfer were a big part of my singing youth and part of me was confident that they would stand the test of time.

On arrival at the club we ordered drinks, settled in and enjoyed a good catch up. As the lights dimmed I was feeling great. I had made the right choice. The atmosphere between us was perfect.

She seemed enthusiastic, relaxed and engaged. The show began. They started with 'Birdland'. An iconic choice. Just what I would have requested. I got straight into it, foot-tapping, head-nodding, rhythm-beating. TMT were on top form. After a few minutes I checked out of the corner of my eye to see if Samira was with me on this.

She was on her iPhone!!

With my hackles rising I launched straight into The 5 Chairs. It went something like this:
Attack Chair. 'What IS she doing? I can't believe this! I go to all this trouble to set up the perfect evening and what does she do? I thought she was different from all the other kids. How ungrateful is that! That is SO disappointing!'

After a good bout of ranting I transitioned into the Hedgehog chair. 'Oh god. How stupid of me. This whole thing was a mistake! She doesn't like TMT. She thinks they are boring and old-fashioned. She probably thinks I am too. What a fool I am. Why didn't I think of something more appropriate for her rather than pushing my own agenda? So typical! Will I ever grow up? This is going to be a disaster.'

Fortunately The Wait Chair came out of the wings in the nick of time. 'Now just a minute Louise. Take it easy. Calm down now. Don't jump to conclusions. Just wait and see what happens. She could be doing anything on her phone. You don't know what's happening in her world right now. Take a deep breath. Have another drink!!'

My Detect voice emerged out of the pause. 'All I want is for us to have a wonderful time together and for her to feel she has a friend in me. Someone she can be herself with. Someone she can turn to when she's in need. That would be such a gift.'

The next voice in my head said 'connect to her needs. The big one!' … blank … 'What's important for her?' … blank again … and I teach this stuff!!'

I was still searching for the answer when TMT stopped playing. As I turned to her with a tentative smile ready for the verdict she looked at me and said,

'Louise, did you know that this is the only Blue Note in Europe. The original one opened in New York in 1981, two in Japan but the fourth one opened here in Milan. Not even in London. Here in Milan! Wow. That's awesome. And I just looked up The Manhattan Transfer. These guys have been performing together for forty years! How do they do that? That's amazing. And look …' She handed me her phone. She'd just sent a message out on Facebook. It said 'In the Blue Note in Milan with Louise. The best!'

We looked at each other and glowed.

A note on
THE 5 CHAIRS ACADEMY

If you feel inspired to practise what you've read, please come and join us at The 5 Chairs Academy where we offer both in-company professional training programmes and personal growth retreats.

Go to *www.the5chairs.com* and stay in touch. I hope to meet you some time in the future.

Appendix

Below is some typical Jackal thinking and talking. Familiarise yourself with the list and then choose an everyday situation at work e.g. attending/running a meeting, taking a decision with a colleague, driving or taking public transport to work, speaking to your boss, negotiating a deal.

Put on your Jackal Detective Hat and watch yourself closely in your chosen situation - like a cat watching a mouse. SPOT - OBSERVE - IDENTIFY and TICK off the Jackals that surface.

TICK	Your BEHAVIOURS / THOUGHTS	JACKAL CATEGORY
	'I'm right'	The Super Judge
	'It's their fault'	The Finger Pointer
	'That's a crazy idea!'	The Super Critic
	'Our approach is better…'	The Comparer
	'You don't know what you're talking about'	The Dismisser
	'It's not my problem'	The Buck Passer
	'He's an idiot'	The Insulter
	'Have you heard the latest…….well…'	The Gossip Monger
	'I refuse to collaborate on that'	The Stonewaller
	'That's not my job'	The Shirker
	'She'll pay for this!'	The Punisher
	'I'm the boss. Just do it!!!'	The Bulldozer
	'I had to do it. I had no choice'	The Renouncer
	'Why does this always happen to me! It's not fair'	The Victim
	'For my eyes only!!'	The Information Hoarder
	'IT people are nerds! The Brits are cold!'	The Condemner
	When you change the 'mood' of a group /situation because of your negative attitude	The Mood Hoover

The Giraffe inspires connection, community, well-being and safety. Its' powerful and determined, yet peaceful and gentle. It's thoughts and behaviours are non-judgmental, non-blaming, non-demanding and non-threatening. It seeks to mitigate conflict and promote peace into the world.

a) Spend a day looking for these Giraffe traits in your colleagues at work
b) Spend time monitoring your own Giraffe behaviours in different work situations

TICK	GIRAFFE THOUGHTS / BEHAVIOURS	GIRAFFE CATEGORY
	'Take your time. I know it's difficult'	The Patient Giraffe
	'You've done a great job for the team. I appreciate your contribution a lot'	The Grateful giraffe
	'What can I do to help you here?'	The Nurturing Giraffe
	'We need to respect the agreement we have drawn up. Doing anything else woud be unethical '	The Ethical Giraffe
	'You've been through a lot just recently. You must be feeling drained'	The Compassionate Giraffe
	'I want to be completely honest with you about this'	The Authentic Giraffe
	'That was my mistake. Sorry. I'll sort it out'	The Responsible Giraffe
	'Could you help me with this? I can't make it work'	The Vulnerable Giraffe
	'What can I do to be a better manager for you?'	The Humble Giraffe
	'I understand your position here'	The Respectful Giraffe
	'I know you haven't done it before but I believe you have what it takes'	The Trusting Giraffe
	'Just let me know whenever you need a hand'	The Kind Giraffe
	'You've been looking tired recently. Take some time to rest'	The Empathetic Giraffe
	' I cut you off when you were speaking. Sorry!'	The Apologetic Giraffe
	'I'll make sure we all have it by tomorrow. Count on me'	The Accountable Giraffe
	'I know you can do it if you want. Take courage and jump in'	The Empowering Graffe
	'We all make mistakes at some time. Let's go over it again'	The Forgiving Giraffe
	'You've got a real talent for this type of sales role. I think you've got a bright future ahead of you'	The Complimentary Giraffe

THE MENTAL DIET
The Ultimate Antidote to Jackal Thinking

This, I can assure you, will be THE most difficult thing you have ever attempted to do in your entire life. Running a full marathon is child's play in comparison. You will probably fail but stay curious. Stay resilient. Don't give up.

It was an Irishman, Emmet Fox, who had the brilliant idea of mental dieting.

The Theory: What is the theory behind a mental diet? Let's consider a few statistics first. Research says that we entertain up to and beyond 70,000 thoughts a day, many of which are subconscious. That's a lot of thought production resulting in about 3000 thoughts per hour and 50 per minute.

Thoughts arise in us as we encounter other people's behaviours or as we meet new situations. They're handed to us through conversation with others, or through the media, social networking and gossip. But how aware am I of what type of thoughts (at least the conscious ones) I'm choosing to entertain on a daily basis? Do I allow my mind to dwell on the negative ones? Can I control my thoughts? Let's investigate.

The Practice: How do we practice a mental diet? This is the hard part. Be prepared for a struggle.

Start listening closely to the chattering voice in your head.
Notice when a thought arrives.
Clearly identify its nature. Is it potentially negative? Is it an emerging Jackal thought?
Once spotted, observe its presence.
Do not judge it, do not entertain it or dwell on it.
Do not get caught up in it.
In other words, do not believe it, fear it or give it power. Just observe it's there.
Then, ACT immediately. Consider the negative thought as a red hot cinder which lands on your sleeve. Flick it off immediately before it burns you.
Now shift your attention.
Invite a positive thought in. For example, notice what's right about the situation or the person. Think about how you can help or contribute and dwell on that.
Repeat this every time a negative thought sneaks in.

As you practise, you will find yourself up against your formidable pack of internal Jackals trying to sabotage any attempts you make at changing your thinking habits. We're carrying years of conditioning with us which don't take kindly to interference, despite all the good intentions we may have.

This practice is strenuous and requires great discipline but don't despair. The biggest problem is remembering to do it in real time. Most of the time we're just not conscious

5 Chairs, 5 Choices

of our own thinking patterns so this diet requires serious mind management. Try it in phases. Try for an hour, then half a day, then a whole day and then seven continuous days, preferably in a relatively stress-free period of your life (holidays?). You will be caught off guard and tempted away from doing it.

But if you persist, the rewards are great. You'll feel lighter. You'll reduce the intake of toxic mental food into your system. You'll be happier, more cheerful. Your life will transform.

Sources of Inspiration

I am truly grateful for the wisdom and inspiration gained from reading the following books:

Dialogue: The Art Of Thinking Together – **William Isaacs**, Doubleday 1999
The New Leadership Paradigm – **Richard Barrett**, 2010
The Inner Game of Tennis – **W. Timothy Gallwey**, Pan Books 1986
A New Earth – **Eckhart Tolle**, Plume 2005
Destructive Emotions – **Daniel Goleman**, Bantam Books 2003
Nonviolent Communication, A Language of Life – **Marshall Rosenberg**, PuddleDancer Press 2005
Man's Search for Meaning – **Viktor E. Frankl**, Rider 1959
Conscious Business – **Fred Kopfman**, Sounds True 2006
A Theory of Everything – **Ken Wilber**, Shambhala 2006
The 7 Habits of Highly Effective People – **Steven Covey**, Simon and Schuster 1989
Hiring for Attitude – **Mark Murphy**, McGraw Hill 2012
The Empathy Factor – **Marie R. Miyashiro**, PuddleDancer Press 2011
Roots of Empathy: Changing the World Child by Child - **Mary Gordon**, Thomas Allen Publishers 2005
From Conflict to Creative Collaboration – **Rosa Zubizarreta**, 2 Harbors 2014
Living Beautifully with Uncertainty and Change – **Pema Chodron**, Shambhala 2013
Daring Greatly – **Brené Brown**, Penguin 2012
Reinventing Organizations – **Federic Laloux**, Nelson Parker 2014

Index

Made in the USA
Middletown, DE
05 June 2019